100 Everyday Epiphanies

Simple Events That
Can Inspire Prayer

100 Everyday Epiphanies

Simple Events That Can Inspire Prayer

To Rita —
Blessings!
Greg Hadley

Greg Hadley

Pleasant Word
A Division of WINEPRESS PUBLISHING

© 2005 by Greg Hadley. All rights reserved.

Pleasant Word (a division of WinePress Publishing, PO Box 428, Enumclaw, WA 98022) functions only as book publisher. As such, the ultimate design, content, editorial accuracy, and views expressed or implied in this work are those of the author.

No part of this publication may be reproduced, stored in a retrieval system or transmitted in any way by any means—electronic, mechanical, photocopy, recording or otherwise—without the prior permission of the copyright holder, except as provided by USA copyright law.

All Scripture references are taken from The New American Bible, Catholic Bible Press, a division of Thomas Nelson Publishers.

ISBN 1-4141-0480-4
Library of Congress Catalog Card Number: 2005903962

Dedication

To My Wife, Evelyn, Always

Table of Contents

Foreword xi
Preface xiii
Acknowledgements xvii

A Walk on the Beach 19
Birth of My First Grandchild 20
Ash Wednesday 21
The Annual Physical Exam 22
Our National Pastime 23
Prostate Specific Antigen 24
The Electric Switch and Faucet 25
Hablando Español 26
The Death of a Young Friend 27
Moss on the Driveway 28
Writing a Letter 29
Family Reunions 30
Driving on Freeways 31
Praying for Dummies 32
The Stations of the Cross 33
A Visit to Honduras 34
Our Flag 35

The "Thank You" Note	36
Building a New Church	37
Thanksgiving Day	38
Singing in the Choir	39
In Line to Receive Communion	40
A Visit to a Senior Center	41
The Triduum	42
Grocery Shopping	43
Writing a Check	44
Taking a Walk	45
My Priest Friends	46
My Business Career	47
Halloween	48
In the Solitude of a Church	49
They're Always Your Children	50
The Personal Computer	51
Serving in the Military	52
Preparing for Winter	53
Guests for Dinner	54
Death of an Old Friend	55
Pain	56
Neighbors	57
A Restaurant Dinner	58
Washing the Car	59
Christmas Lights	60
A Visit from Grandchildren	61
On Being a Eucharistic Minister	62
Wrapping a Present	63
Watching Television	64
Cooking	65
An Argument with a Friend	66
Home Repairs	67
A New Pastor	68
The Sunday Collection	69
The Perfect Day	70
On Being Fired	71

The Greeting Card	72
Christmas Gift Shopping	73
The Garage Attic	74
The Parish Fundraising Committee	75
Choosing Life	76
Compassion	77
Loneliness	78
The Big Mistake	79
The Hospital Waiting Room	80
The First Tee	81
My "Geezer" Friends	82
My Brother	83
My Sister	84
My Wife	85
Praying the Rosary	86
The Telephone Answering Machine	87
The Automobile Accident	88
Sitting on the Front Porch	89
Coffee and Donuts	90
Wealth	91
Mail Delivery	92
Remodeling	93
The Mountains	94
The Rivers	95
My Calendar Book	96
The Cleaning Ladies	97
The Comic Strips	98
Our Family Scrapbooks	99
"A Bottle of Wine, a Piece of Bread . . ."	100
The Backyard Barbecue	101
Auto Repairs	102
Pentecost	103
Summer Vacation	104
My Women Friends	105
Work after Retirement	106
Public Speaking	107

My Mother and My Father	108
A Teenager Learning to Drive	109
Baby's First Steps	110
Elation!	111
Rejection	112
The Airplane Trip	113
Wedding Anniversaries	114
The Capacity of a Child to Hurt	115
Habits	116
Rainbows	117
Where Do I Go From Here?	118

Foreword

Several years ago a Midwestern woman came to Portland to visit her daughter. One morning while her daughter was at work, the woman went to Mt. Hood for a hike to beautiful McNeil Point. She did not return. The mountain search unit looked for her for four days and three nights. Late on the fourth day, our team descended into the Muddy Fork Canyon, our assigned search area. On the bank of the stream we found some footprints. Moments later we found the woman 150 yards up the canyon. As we checked her physical condition, my eyes met one of the other team members. We were both crying. It was so wonderful that she was alive!

What you have in your hands is a little book that celebrates being alive. It celebrates life! Almost everyone, even small children, will tell you that living is often difficult and filled with problems, issues, concerns, worries and challenges. But *life?* Ah, life is great! Life is where we can see and touch and feel and hear and smell the roses. Life is where we can grow and learn and reach out for the possible and dream of the impossible. Life is where we ponder the wonder of our planet and this universe. Life is when we let our own intellects be a part of the creative process. But the best thing about life is that we can love. It's no small matter, this loving and being in love.

Every human being on the planet represents an epiphany. Our birth, our first appearance, the initial manifestation that we are here, means that anything is potential. From this moment on, the world will be a better *or a worse* place because of us. The sages say that we are the Creator's gift; what we become is our gift back to the Creator. Strange as it may seem, the shaping of that gift will probably not take place primarily in the spectacular events of our lives. It will happen largely in the small, insignificant things we do. It will be the gentle care that we take of the world and the people all around us. It will be in the open mind we present toward opportunity. It will be in the open heart that touches many unknown to us. And when the Creator accepts our gift, we will respond in wonder at our own peace.

I do not think of myself as a religious person. I know that I am a loving person and that loving has a way of making life a prayer. As I've made my way through this book, the thought has kept coming to me: "Yes, that's how it felt—that chance I was given to understand life more clearly wasn't missed." Maybe to the religious person this simply means *to cooperate with God's grace.* Grace is said to be all around us, all the time, and in everything. As Greg has said so well, "In the simple things I shall keep looking for Him."

Hugh O'Reilly
Tualatin, Oregon.

Preface

This is a prayer book written by an old man.

Well past seventy, I hope that the years have imparted some level of wisdom to me, but I'm not convinced of that. Actually, I sometimes feel less sure of myself now than when I was younger. I have been around long enough to know that my encounters with God are not usually the result of lightning bolts, thunder claps, eclipses of the sun, or burning bushes in the desert. People I know talk about "life altering epiphanies" in their own lives. For some it is a weekend religious retreat conducted by an inspiring preacher. Others will say that observing a spectacular event like an erupting volcano profoundly changed them. Perhaps a critical illness or reading a special book has turned you around. Most will give you a blank stare if you ask them about epiphanies in their own lives. They haven't had one, at least not an event they're aware of as such, or are willing to think about and discuss.

I have had only one *big epiphany* in my lifetime. I attended a weekend session with a group of men in November 1969 called a *Cursillo* (translated from Spanish, it means, "a short course.") For those of you who have been on a Cursillo retreat, you probably know exactly what I mean. For the rest, it would take another book to explain what one experiences in those three short days. The effect on me was breathtaking. I have told many that I was a Roman Catholic all my life but the Cursillo converted me to being a Christian Roman Catholic. There is a big difference between those two descriptions, in my opinion.

This book is about simple, mundane, and everyday events that have led me to prayer. Please do not conclude that I am a great, persistent, and devoted person who has irrevocably turned his life over to God. Far from it. My struggles with the sins of bad temper, selfishness, and other faults too numerous (and embarrassing) to name, weigh me down. Because I was blessed with a total Catholic education—Sisters of St. Joseph of Carondelet nuns for grammar school, Christian Brothers for high school, and Jesuits for university—I *know* God's teaching and what kind of a life I am supposed to live. My problem is I don't always act as I should. As St. Luke writes in Chapter 12, verse 48, "Much will be required of the person entrusted with much, and still more will be demanded of the person entrusted with more." I am constantly haunted by that phrase because I have been given so much during my lifetime.

Reflecting on my life, I have found that I am personally led to God more by run-of-the-mill, common things that many of us experience in our lives. The *big epiphany* is easy to remember and is etched on our spirits. But, I believe many will find God in the everyday give-and-take of life. I have always sought a balance in my prayers between *adoration* of God, *contrition* for my sins, *thanksgiving* for all the blessings given to me, and *supplication* for the things that I, and others, need. Thinking about the simple events of life helps me to keep the balanced prayer life I am seeking.

God is always reaching out to us. While He loves us unconditionally, I think He also wants us to respond to Him as often as we can. I don't believe our personal prayer model always has to be drop-to-your-knees, fold your hands, and lift your eyes to heaven. Sure, sometimes that is called for. But most of the time we merely can say:

"Father God, I can feel Your Presence in that sunset,
a walk along the beach, the turn of a faucet that produces hot
    water,
or my neighbor whom I greeted today. I hope to find You
in equally simple things tomorrow, too.
Thank You, God, for being ever-present to me in this way."

I could be wrong but I think this is a very acceptable response to My Creator, one He is looking for.

I was able to think of one hundred everyday epiphanies that led me to God. You will find them in the following pages. I'm quite sure you can think of many more, and better, epiphanies from your daily experiences.

I hope this little book, written in the late autumn of my life, may inspire you to seek new and simple ways to respond to God's love. I comment that "no one goes to heaven by him or herself." It would be wonderful if this book provided some help to you so we could walk, hand in hand, toward the Promised Land. I pray fervently that you get there. Will you please pray that I make it, too? *Thanks.* I hope to meet you there in time.

Acknowledgements

I find it incongruous that someone like me should write what is essentially a prayer book. I think I am being presumptuous to believe that I could inspire someone to respond to God in prayer by what I have composed. This is not a case of false modesty seeking praise. I think God has allowed me to know myself pretty well. What I sometimes see is not very pretty. Yes, God has blessed me abundantly and through His graces I have tried to lead a pious and religious life to the best of my ability. However, I have often failed. If the Roman Catholic Church is a refuge for sinners, I am definitely in the right place. To keep the virtue of Hope alive within me, I have great trust in God's mercy toward sinners like myself.

I did feel called to write this small book. No great wind blew through my room, waking me up and whispering to me, "Start writing." It was just something I felt I could do well. You will decide whether or not that assessment was correct. A lifetime of Catholic education, active involvement in my parishes, and teaching The Rite of Christian Initiation of Adults (RCIA) for fourteen years exposed me to much church dogma and various forms of prayer. Along the way I was inspired by my brother's unwavering Christian life and the difficulty my sister overcame with the Catholic Church and her return to full communion. My wife, Evelyn, has been a constant beacon to me, showing how a diverse and persistent prayer life can sustain a person. Others crossed my path, leading me to a deeper understanding of my faith and showing me how much

God loves me. Included in that group were Brother Anselm, FSC, Coach Mike Karbo, Father James Lyons, S.J., Father Emmett McCarthy, Father Enrique Parisi, OFM, and Father John Kerns. Many others came into my life and uplifted me, including Briegeen Moore, Sarah Shrewsbury, "Bud" Clark, "Pancho" Holcomb, Fred Von Voigt, and Al Shammel. My religious awakening was aided by many friends in Oregon, including Sheryle Kaluza, Bob Hammers, Theo Roche, Carol DeJardin, Lois and Dick Street, Hugh and Dawn O'Reilly, Joan LeBarron, Geri Schub, Gail and Christine Boyd, Pat Walsh, and Father Dick Rossman. Literally hundreds of others have had a positive influence on me. I wish I could remember and list all their names, but that is not possible. Thank you, each and every one.

To God the Father, God the Son, and God the Holy Spirit, I can only say an inadequate "thank you" for the graces poured out on me during my lifetime. I dedicate this book to those both known and unknown to me who need to feel the unconditional love, joy, and mercy of our God.

A Walk on the Beach

I'm very lucky. I have visited many wonderful places. My feet have walked on beautiful beaches in Hawaii, Fiji, Australia, New Zealand, Ireland, and Mexico. In this great country, I've been to the shorelines of oceans, big rivers, and numerous lakes. Whether the surf is pounding or just gently lapping the shore, nothing is quite as lovely as a leisurely stroll on a sandy beach.

Think of the billions and billions of grains of sand that comprise a beach. It is beyond our comprehension to differentiate one grain from another. And yet, that is exactly what God does as He watches over each of us, His human creatures.

"Before you were born, your name was carved in the palm of My hand," says our Creator. (Isaiah 49: 16). "I know the number of hairs on your head," He tells us. (Matthew 10:30)

Incredible! I try to imagine how much unconditional love He must have for me! Why is this fact so hard for me to comprehend?

"Father God, I pray…
Billions of souls have come before me.
Billions more will follow after me.
I am merely a grain of sand on an infinite beach.
My existence seems so insignificant.
But not so to You, my God. I am but a tiny speck, but Your love for me is infinite!
I praise and worship You, Mighty Creator."

Birth of My First Grandchild

We were on a driving vacation. At the end of the day, we checked for messages on our home answering machine. Our oldest son, Bing, had called. His wife, Laura, had gone into labor and was now in the hospital preparing to give birth. This was to be our first grandchild.

Like all grandparents, we considered the event something very special. Since our trip was flexible, we changed course and headed directly toward the location where the birth would take place. We arrived the next day and wondrously held our tiny granddaughter in our arms. Little Sarah represented our posterity, our immortality, a link to our heritage and a bridge to the future. *She is an incredible new creature of God!* I thought, silently.

How can the merging of a tiny egg and minute sperm result in such a wondrous creature? God is an awesome God!

> "Father God, I pray…
> Sometimes I turn away from You, my God.
> At times, I have even questioned Your existence.
> But Your handiwork, Lord, is so magnificent.
> I am compelled to return to You.
> How can I reject You after seeing a baby?
> I am stunned when I see the greatness of creation.
> I must prostrate myself in adoration. You are an awesome God!"

Ash Wednesday

Ash Wednesday, the first day of the Lenten season, is unique in the liturgical life of the Church. After Vatican II, the signs and symbols of faith became richer and reminded me more clearly about the ultimate purpose of my life. The dark cross of ashes signed on our foreheads is both sobering and full of hope.

"Remember, man, you are dust and to dust you shall return." (Genesis 4:19)

Jesus spent forty days in the desert before starting His public ministry. Lent gives me a chance to go to my own desert place for prayer, fasting, and almsgiving. In weakness I would like to turn away from this opportunity. Cutting back on food and drink and abstaining from meat on Fridays seems "old fashioned" and irrelevant in today's culture. I avoid carrying my crosses. But, I have learned that mine are lighter than the one carried by Jesus and those borne by many of my friends.

"I need to be reminded of this fact daily, Lord. Thank you for today's cross and ashes."

> *"Father God, I pray…*
> *Death is so decisive.*
> *Even the faithful Christian is sobered by the thought of it.*
> *I am now in the late autumn of my life.*
> *I begin to count my last Lenten seasons.*
> *I number the final Easter celebrations.*
> *Help me to focus on resurrection, not death.*
> *Give me trust in Your love and mercy, Lord.*
> *Remind me often that Good Friday was not the end.*
> *It was followed by Easter Sunday."*

The Annual Physical Exam

I'm faithful about scheduling an annual physical exam. At my age it is just prudent to make sure all systems are working properly. I know a lot of men who say, "I'm feeling great—why should I see a doctor?" Good luck to them, but I think this is a risky position.

I've been blessed with pretty good health throughout my life. Still, I have a sense of apprehension as the date of the exam approaches. Have those added pounds increased my blood pressure? Does that little change in my heart rhythm mean anything? When the tests are completed, will the doctor tell me all is well...*or not?* Someday, will I hear these words: "There is a problem we need to talk about. Can you come into my office right away?"

Am I prepared for the final stage of life's journey? Will I still trust in the Lord when death must be faced?

> "Father God, I pray...
> I profess to love and trust You,
> But I dread losing control over my own life.
> Why am I so reluctant to turn everything over to You?
> Please teach me to say,
> "Into Your hands I commend my spirit." (Luke 23:46)
> Jesus did that.
> So must I."

Our National Pastime

Baseball is the perfect game. Many have referred to it as an art form. I agree. Since its inception, the rules of baseball have changed very little. The distance between the bases, the size and shape of the field, and how far the pitcher must throw the ball continue to be a perfect test of the athletes. Most plays in a game are close and exciting. I can identify with the players, who are mostly average-sized people…not like the giants of basketball or football.

The passage of this game is marked by turns at bat, not time. There is hope for victory even if you have only one more chance to score. Baseball is a metaphor for our own existence. Even in the late stages of life's journey, we have time left. We can still do what is necessary to make our lives successful in the eyes of God.

I'm trying to use my final "outs" as best I can. In spite of errors made earlier in the game of life, there is still time to secure victory in the final inning. I'm still "at bat" and swinging.

> "Father God, I pray…
> Help me to see that I still have some time.
> I know that soon the 'game' will be over.
> Let me use each moment You've given to me productively.
> Lead me to reconcile with family and friends.
> Even in 'the last of the ninth' let me keep trying.
> Then I can leave the field having done my best.
> I want to be eligible for Your 'Hall of Fame.'"

Prostate Specific Antigen

PSA. Prostate Specific Antigen. This simple blood test, along with a doctor's examination, can assist in determining if a man has prostate cancer. My father died of this disease so I have been careful about getting a yearly check for it. Recently my low PSA reading spiked higher. I sought the advice of a specialist. Further testing, including a biopsy, determined that I had cancer. I underwent surgery to remove the prostate. Often this produces a cure. In my case, some of the tumor had already escaped the capsule of the gland. I now face an uncertain future.

I've always tried to be in control of the events of my life. A little blood test gave me a jarring reminder that *I* was not the one in charge. *Why did I spend so much time trying to show God that I was in control, not He?*

"Some of life's lessons can be very hard to accept, Lord."

"Father God, I pray...
I turn to You when things go wrong.
It's easy, then, to get on my knees, to seek Your aid.
'Heal me! Solve my problem!' I plead.
Instead, I should have asked: 'Let me trust...'
Now, I have no choice.
I must turn it over to You.
Give me the grace of humility.
Lead me where I am to go.
To trust is hard. I need Your help to do it."

The Electric Switch and Faucet

Without thought I enter my home using an automatic garage door opener. Once inside, I flip a switch to turn on lights, increase the thermostat to warm the house, draw hot water to wash my hands, open the fridge to check for snacks, and sit down to watch television. Nothing in this typical homecoming routine gives me one second of amazement. It should.

How much I take for granted in my daily life! I turn a key, my car starts. I operate a switch and electricity flows. A turn of a handle that produces hot water or cool, clean water for drinking. Buses and trains run (mostly) on schedule. Traffic signals work. Elevators go up and down safely. Supermarkets are stocked with food. Given time, I could think of hundreds of similar examples.

I don't think things work that way in rural China or in darkest Africa. Why am I not more appreciative for these simple blessings?

"Father God, I pray…
I am abundantly blessed with material riches.
Conveniences and gadgets make my life easier.
Help me to see Your Hand in all these wondrous things.
Let me understand how comfortable and easy my life is.
I take so much for granted daily.
These things are remarkable luxuries to others.
Teach me to be thankful for everything I have."

Hablando Español

Most of my adult life I have wanted to speak Spanish. Working in California, I had extensive interaction with Hispanics. At the companies I managed, the majority of employees were Spanish-speaking. I wanted to communicate with them casually and easily on a daily basis. I took many classes to obtain a basic grasp of the language. My success was marginal. I could speak OK, but my ears never got trained to interpret the rapid-fire Spanish spoken to me. Even after retiring, I took a three-week language immersion class in Mexico. I learned a lot but still do not converse fluently.

I found that it's tough to communicate with someone who speaks a different language. But what of my family, friends, and neighbors, who all speak the same language? I find that there is often a similar difficulty in communicating effectively, even with them.

Is communication not the hardest thing a human does? Why do I misspeak to others so often—or misinterpret what they say to me?

> "Father God, I pray...
> So often I find myself misunderstanding something another said.
> I misinterpret communication meant for me.
> I understand the words but not their meaning.
> I take offense when none was intended.
> Sometimes I speak out in hurtful ways, too.
> Help me to communicate gently, respectfully.
> Dip in honey both the words I speak and those that I hear."

The Death of a Young Friend

I met Peter at church. He was twenty-eight years old. We sang in the choir together. He was tall, slim, and handsome, possessing a ready smile and a wry sense of humor. Along with his wife, Barbara, and their little daughter, Lili, they represented the all-American family in every way.

Sadly, this young baritone contracted Hodgkin's disease. He battled and defeated it for a while, but like a midnight fog it crept silently back. God claimed Peter in His own time. His funeral liturgy was a true celebration of life. The oldest of nine children, Peter had been an inspiration to his siblings. He was not only loved but admired.

I hate it when young people die. Somehow it seems like things are out of order. Old people should die and be buried by the young ones.

There I go again, telling God how things are supposed to be.

"*Father God, I pray…*
Death often distorts the normal course of life.
Help me to accept that Your will is accomplished.
My clouded human mind cannot fathom a reason.
Why have You let this happen to my friend?
I want to rebel against Your will.
Show me how to surrender.
Teach me to pray: 'Thy will be done.'"

Moss on the Driveway

A typical winter full of Oregon rain will leave a telltale coating of slippery, unattractive green moss on my walks and driveways. The stuff grows everywhere. It's hard to get rid of, too. Each spring I'm off to the rental yard to get a pressure sprayer. It takes a lot of force to dislodge the moss. If you become impatient and skip some places, the moss almost smiles at you. Glistening in the sun, it defiantly lets you know, "You missed me! I'm staying right here so I can continue to grow and bother you all summer long!"

The moss is like some of my own familiar behaviors and habits. My interaction with loved ones, friends, and passers-by can become slippery and unattractive. I find this behavior very hard for me to get rid of! Even after scolding myself when I have been unkind or hurtful, I find that I am doing it again a short time later. God must want to take a divine *pressure washer* to me sometimes and clean me up for company. I wouldn't blame Him if He did, either!

I hope to have a nice, moss-free driveway next spring. Submitting to God's good maintenance plan, I'll try to keep my soul in the same condition, as well.

"Father God, I pray...
My weak human nature attracts ugly moss.
No matter how hard I try, I fail too often.
I seem to have a reservoir of unkindness.
Where do these dark moods originate?
Why do I find myself often wounding those I love?
Pressure wash me, Lord!
I need it badly."

Writing a Letter

We used to write letters, but not so much anymore. Faxes, emails, and the rising cost of postage have accelerated this trend away from expressing ourselves with pen or pencil. The fast pace of our too-busy lives is a major factor, as well. It really is too bad.

What can brighten spirits more than finding a letter in the mailbox from an old friend or family member? When one arrives, I sit down and savor every word. I read of good news, exciting news, or sadness between the lines—a relationship broken, an opportunity lost, or an imminent tragedy. I read the letter several times to make sure every meaning is gleaned, the nuance of every word deciphered.

The decline in letter writing may be a metaphor for things happening in our society. Old-timers like me are nostalgic for the "good old days" when life seemed gentler, more orderly, less filled with tension and anxiety. I don't stand in the way of progress. I just wish we didn't have to abandon so many things along the pathways of today's culture and life to get there.

I want to embrace the new, but hold on to the good, old things, too.

> "Father God, I pray.
> Help me to see the bright promise in all things new.
> I do want to embrace the future.
> Show me how to link it up with the past.
> Let me see the glorious possibilities that change can bring.
> I am often mired in things long past.
> I whine about all these unfamiliar new ways.
> In those moments, show me Your love that never changes."

Family Reunions

We have a longstanding tradition of getting together with our six children, their spouses, and our grandchildren once a year. We call it "Camp Hadley." It is quite an event, usually lasting four to five days and including nearly forty people in all, depending on what guests show up.

Circumstances may keep some away, but usually all assemble in a common location for play, conversation, shared meals, and the latest stories. Most of us live in different areas so everyone looks forward to the chance for catch up with all the family members. While usually fun, there is the occasional dust-up that may ruffle someone's feathers. But love always seems to prevail and things smooth out before long.

The love between siblings, their spouses, and the grandchildren is a marvel to me. Even the little outbursts or unkind words are followed by a hug and kiss. Watching my children love one another is a huge return on the investment made in parenting them.

> "Father God, I pray…
> You tell us to love one another.
> To do so, we must act the same way toward each other that You act toward us.
> Easy to say, often hard to do.
> Oh, it's not too difficult to love your own, but we are called to love our extended families,
> even the ones that are especially hard to love.
> Show me how to do that, Lord."

Driving on Freeways

In my youth the nuns at grammar school taught me about "the near occasions of sin." These were people, places, or things that provided us temptations to offend God. Driving on the freeways is often a "near occasion" for me. I have no tolerance for the incredibly stupid, invincibly ignorant, and enormously thoughtless people who share the road with me. They either drive too fast or too slow. They change lanes without signaling. They cut in front of me and routinely annoy me with their senseless antics. I, of course, am always a careful and competent driver. Just ask me; I'll be pleased to tell you.

Naturally I let these people know about their transgressions in no uncertain terms. My gestures, shouts, a blaring horn and flicking high beams let these miscreants know I am not to be trifled with.

Whoa! What kind of self-righteous deception am I playing on myself? These other drivers are my neighbors! Where is my self-control? Where is my Christian charity? Where is my patience?

Heaven, help us!

"Father God, I pray…
Why do I see the speck in my neighbor's eye so clearly?
Yet I cannot see the plank in my own.
The Human Condition makes me frequently thoughtless.
I become careless with the rights and feelings of others.
I call them to account and demand their perfection,
But I am subject to great imperfection myself.
Help me to be patient and nonjudgmental."

Praying for Dummies

In recent years there have been numerous books written "for dummies." These texts are intended to make certain complex subjects understandable to those of us not possessing the skills to grasp them. Most of these books relate to the ubiquitous personal computer, whose jargon and complexity often flummox those lacking a technical background. It is disconcerting to be described as a "dummy," but I admit that some of these manuals *are* often helpful as I struggle to operate my own computer.

Someone should write a book entitled *Praying for Dummies*. I don't spend nearly enough time praying. *Why?* I often find I am not too comfortable communicating with my Creator. Sometimes I will fall back on "formula" prayers found in some book or pamphlet. Does God always hear me? Am I supposed to talk, or listen? What if I don't get what I have prayed for?

I want to pray better but, let's face it, this *dummy* could use some help.

> *"Father God, I pray…*
> *I often avoid doing things I don't do well.*
> *There is such a gulf between my human nature and Your Divine Person.*
> *Teach me that You are present to me always.*
> *Let me understand that You eagerly seek me out.*
> *Listen to my simple prayers when I offer them.*
> *Remind me that even "dummies" are heard when they speak in earnest."*

The Stations of the Cross

The Way of the Cross has always been a favorite devotion during Lenten Season. The variety of reflections continues to make the story of Jesus' last few hours of human life profoundly awesome to me, no matter how many times it is told. Each of the fourteen Stations reveals something about courage, patience, love, sacrifice, forgiveness, endurance of pain and, finally, acceptance and death.

The characters described in the Stations intrigue me. I'm especially interested in Simon, the Cyrene. This foreigner was forced by the guards to help Jesus carry His cross. Why not a friend or disciple? No, Jesus wanted the help of someone unknown, a stranger. As I walk along my road of life, there are many "Simons" willing to assist me, but too often I ignore them.

Lord, let me seek out those who can help me. Teach me to accept the outstretched hands of others. It is hard to accept help from others, especially strangers, but give me humility to do so.

> "Father God, I pray:
> I am humbled by Your Son's overwhelming love for me.
> His constant caring touches my heart and soul.
> He suffered the agony of death on a cross.
> This He accepted willingly to save all mankind.
> Help me to share His story with all I meet.
> And make sure, Lord that I receive my 'Simons' along the way."

A Visit to Honduras

In January 2004 my wife and I visited our "sister parish" in rural Honduras. Before the trip we spent time visiting medical travel clinics in order to get necessary immunizations and medicines. The shots and pills were just minor inconveniences. However, they did cause us to ask, "What are we getting into?"

The last air leg of our trip was Houston to Tegucigalpa. It could be compared to landing on the moon. We found ourselves in a place so different from home we could scarcely believe it. For the next ten days we lived with bottled water, impassable roads, cold showers, and insects. Yet all the people we encountered were warm, loving, interested in us, happy, and filled with abiding faith. This, in spite of wrenching poverty everywhere we turned. We left after our short visit humbled and deeply moved. Inevitably, we asked one another: "Why were we born in the United States instead of Honduras?"

Your ways are unfathomable, O Lord.

> "Father God, I pray…
> I know that all people are members of the Body of Christ.
> All of the billions of us are inextricably linked through Your Incarnation.
> But why are some of us so incredibly blessed—and others born into a life
>   of deprivation?
> Show me the ways to thank You for the awesome blessings You have given
>   to me."

Our Flag

According to flag etiquette, *Old Glory* should be displayed at half-mast until noon on Memorial Day and then raised fully for the balance of the day. I love to see our flag fluttering in the breeze. It's a beautiful collage of symbols depicting our country's history.

When I was a boy I was fascinated by the colorful collection of many countries' flags in our encyclopedia. *Why were they designed that way? What did the various symbols mean? Who decided what colors to use?* The flags of many countries around the world looked much the same, but the flag of the United States of America was unique.

Those living in the shadow of each country's flag are often quite different in language, heritage, custom, and culture. But are the world's people really so different? The church hymn, "One Bread, One Body" written by Rev. John Foley, S. J., says it well: "Gentile or Jew, servant or free, woman or man no more. We, though many, throughout the world are one body in the One Lord."

Amen!

"Father God, I pray.
I proclaim solidarity with my brothers and sisters.
But, do I really mean it?
You said, 'Love one another.'
OK, I will do that—but certainly not all.
There are those who hate me and want to hurt me.
I don't want to love them, Lord.
Because I am weak, will You love them for me, please?"

The "Thank You" Note

When our children were little we made them sit down and write "thank you" notes to grandparents and friends after Christmas and birthdays. Yes, there was resistance.

"I don't know what to say!" was the cry. Well, we said, just say "thank you" for the gift and tell them how much you are enjoying it. We wanted to instill a sense of common courtesy in our kids and an appreciation for what had been given to them. It seems to have stuck. They are passing this along to their children, as well. But we are not seeing this so much with many others in the next generation. Truthfully, this really annoys me.

Too often my friends tell me about gifts they have sent to their children or grandchildren that are never acknowledged. Often one feels lucky to get a cryptic text message email saying "thx 4 the $." I am probably guilty of this, too. Sure, I say "thanks" to family, friends, and neighbors who give me something or do things for me. But what about the countless blessings I receive from God each day? Is my prayer too full of "Help me, Lord," and "Give me, Lord," yet lacking in "Thank you, Lord."

Is God annoyed, too, because I lack a sense of appreciation?

> "Father God, I pray…
> I am unaware of most of the blessings You give me each day.
> I just take for granted the next breath, the steady heartbeat.
> My very existence depends on Your will.
> My health, my wealth, my talents, my skills.
> All these things come from You.
> Make me constantly aware of the untold blessings You send.
> Make 'thank you' the most important part of my prayer.
> In my weakness, I need Your grace to make this happen."

Building a New Church

We had been worshipping for almost ten years in a converted stable and our parish needed a new church building. It fell upon me as the new Chair of our Pastoral Council to organize the debate, gain consensus, and make the fateful and expensive decision to move forward. My background and experience suited me well for this job, so I did not shirk the responsibility. But, the whole process turned out to be more difficult, time consuming, and emotional than I'd ever anticipated.

There were many *naysayers* and skeptics. We expected this. Some were constantly critical about design issues. Others were terrified of committing their time and treasure to the project. But that wasn't my biggest problem. I found out that I trusted my skills and persuasiveness too much. I relied on the Holy Spirit too little.

After a long and difficult journey of three years we occupied our beautiful, contemporary, new church building. As I sat in the magnificent edifice on Dedication Day, I came to understand it was the Hand of the Spirit that completed the task, not the frail, weak, human hands of my colleagues and me.

> "Father God, I pray…
> Send the Holy Spirit to touch my heart and spirit.
> Fill me with trust and humility.
> Show me that self-reliance is a mistake based on pride.
> Remind me that it is only through You that I can succeed.
> Teach me that any gifts I have are on loan from You.
> Help me not to be judgmental of those who disagree with me."

Thanksgiving Day

The fourth Thursday in November represents many different things. Some people are reminded of the initial celebration of our Pilgrim forefathers as they gave thanks for the harvest and for their survival. To others it is a day of gorging on turkey, dressing, pumpkin pie—and enjoying football games. For those in the retail business, it is the last day before the mad crush of Christmas shoppers seeking perfect gifts begins.

I wonder why we have just one day set aside to say "thank you" for our abundant blessings... Have we turned into a society where "thanks" is often forgotten? Are we like the ten lepers Jesus cured? Do you recall that only one returned to give thanks? (Luke 17: 11-19). Most of us have become so blasé about our abundance that we take it for granted. *Big mistake!* Spend a couple of weeks in a third world country to sharpen your perception of how blessed all of us are.

Why don't most of us catch on to this? I wonder. Are we like those nine lepers?

"Father God, I pray...
I raise my very best prayer to You.
I love You, love You, love You.
I'm sorry, sorry, sorry.
Help me, help me, help me.
Thank You, thank You, thank You.
Without Your unending aid, what of any value would my life contain?"

Singing in the Choir

I love to sing in the choir. I've been singing in it most of my life, even though I can't read music. I have been gifted with a fairly strong tenor voice. I figure if God was willing to lend me this talent, the least I could do was use it. Sometimes I am the Cantor and enjoy leading the congregation in song during liturgical celebrations.

I have often been told that *when we sing we pray twice.* Occasionally I am disappointed when I look out into the congregation and observe someone who is not joining in the singing. I try to cut them some slack; maybe they're embarrassed. Perhaps they feel they couldn't carry a tune in a bucket. But that's not the point. I believe God is happy if we sing loudly, even if we have lousy voices.

Developing a church choir is a difficult job. Most people in the pews don't realize how hard choirs work! It's not easy to take a bunch of volunteers and blend their talents into angelic sounds that will touch our hearts and inspire our worship.

Of course, there are a lot of ways to praise God. Singing is just one twice-blessed way.

> *"Father God, I pray...*
> *Sometimes I talk to You from my knees. Sometimes the Bible inspires my prayer.*
> *I may sense You and speak to You as I walk along the pathways of my neighborhood.*
> *Doing my best in the choir is praise to You.*
> *Help me to always see that there are many ways to pray."*

In Line to Receive Communion

It is a sacred time of Mass when the congregation approaches the altar to receive the Lord Jesus under the form of bread and wine. Through faith, we Catholics believe we are receiving not bread and wine but the Body, Blood, soul and divinity of Jesus Christ. Just the thought of taking the Body of Christ in your hand and drinking His blood from the cup is almost too awesome to contemplate.

And yet for most it is easy to become distracted when receiving Holy Communion. Proceeding in line, my mind wanders. *There's my neighbor, John. I haven't seen him in a while. I wonder if Mrs. Smith knows that her slip is showing. Bill Brown sure is putting on weight....*

Suddenly, I'm at the head of the line. I take the host, then the cup, and return to my pew, trying to remember the words to the song the choir is singing. I have had a personal encounter with God that may have become a wasted moment for me.

Why is this breathtaking moment often lost on me? How can I focus my heart and soul on Jesus when He comes?

> "Father God, I pray.
> If I were in the presence of a king or queen, president or movie star—
> I would be riveted on them. But when I am with You, I often lose my focus.
> Help me to be aware of Your Presence in the sacred host and chalice.
> It represents the Bread of Life and the Cup of Salvation for me.
> Help me to worthily receive You each Sunday morning as You come."

A Visit to a Senior Center

My wife and I often visit residents of senior centers. When we were younger, we felt our presence brought solace, friendship, and compassion to these folks. Of course, we also carried the Lord in Holy Communion. This was the most important part of our visit. We often observed a subtle physical change when people received the Eucharist. Over time we came to know and love many of our aging friends and were saddened when they eventually passed away.

Not all of the visits were enjoyable. Seeing people with severe dementia and dignity-destroying illnesses is hard to deal with on a human level. It is difficult to conduct a pleasant visit with someone lying in a soiled bed who gives little indication of being aware of your presence. After our visits, Evie and I marveled at the work of Mother Teresa and her nuns, who faced these grim encounters constantly.

Now we're not so youthful and sometimes find ourselves dealing with folks younger than we are. As we age, each new visit reminds us of a powerful reality: we are looking at the face of Jesus in every person we see. The Lord said, "Whatever you do for one of these least ones, you do to Me." (Matthew 25: 40). Thank you for the moments when we can touch You in this intimate way.

> "Father God, I pray…
> We, too, ache and creak now.
> But we can still visit our frail, elderly, and infirm.
> Help us to do this work without complaint.
> As we look at the wrinkled faces of others,
> Show us Your loving Face in each person visited.
> As we offer Eucharist to our aged friends,
> Help us to properly reflect the Love we bring."

The Triduum

Every year during Holy Week I've received deepening spiritual insight about the unconditional love God has for each of us. Especially during the Triduum—the three consecutive days of Holy Thursday, Good Friday, and The Easter Vigil—I consciously open my heart and mind as I listen to God's ancient story of love and sacrifice for us. There is a seamless story told over these three days about Jesus establishing the Eucharist for us, subjecting Himself to unspeakable agony leading to death, and then making it all meaningful by the act of His Resurrection. The words we hear and the ceremonies we observe may be repetitious, but the message is continuously fresh and inspiring. *How much God must love us!* I am humbled by the thought of it.

The real question is this: *How do I possibly respond to God's infinite love with my weak, finite spirit?* No matter what I do to try and love God in return, I encounter my ragged, soiled life. It is enough to cause great discouragement, which I have felt. But then I hear God say to me, "I do not seek your human perfection; I seek your effort to love Me and your neighbors. Do your best."

Thank God for His merciful hand on my imperfect life!

> "Father God, I pray…
> First You shared Your Body and Blood with Your friends.
> Then You showed them Your perfect humanness.
> You asked the Father to relieve You of this agony.
> Accepting Your fate, You suffered the cruelest of tortures—even death on
>   a cross!
> I rejoice in Your Resurrection, confirming Your mission.
> What have I done to deserve this unbelievable love?
> Nothing. Thank you, God, for loving me."

Grocery Shopping

My wife is a "professional" grocery shopper. She knows the price of everything, carefully clips and uses discount coupons, and knows just the place to find the best fish or fresh vegetables. I, on the other hand, shop like a typical male. I know what I want, resolutely proceed through the store until my list is completed, and check out as quickly as possible. I don't even know the prices of things I have put into my cart. I seldom compare brands. No wonder I'm surprised how little I seem to get for the money I spend!

Have you ever purchased food in another country? Often the selection is limited, fresh fruits and vegetables look wilted and colorless, prices are high relative to the local economy, and competition is virtually nonexistent. The choices for acquiring nutritious food in Mexico, Central America, Asia, and Africa are often bleak and limited. So, when I shop I try to remember my brothers and sisters in far off lands and how *they* must shop to feed their families.

It's much too easy to become complacent with my abundance.

"Father God, I pray…
So many people struggle daily to obtain basic human needs.
Where will they find food, shelter, and clothing?
What can I do to be in solidarity with them?
I cannot solve the world's hunger problem on my own.
I cannot build houses or provide clothes for all of them.
Perhaps I can find creative ways to help one or two others in need.
Help me, Lord, to do something—anything—to help.
Show me how to share Your love one person at a time."

Writing a Check

I find it comforting to find a healthy balance in my checkbook at month's end. Throughout my life, I have been blessed with good jobs providing excellent income and the chance to save for retirement. While not rich, my wife and I have almost never felt a pinch regarding money. We know some who worry from paycheck to paycheck. *Where are the funds going to come from to pay the property taxes, the braces for the kid's teeth, or the needed repairs to the house?* This kind of constant worry can weary the soul.

There is a different kind of problem faced by those with some level of affluence. It can be equally damaging to the soul. It is materialism. I am constantly bombarded by the media about my "need" for more and more things. A bigger house, a fancier car, a vacation home, ski trips, European travel, more electronic gadgets…. I'm told I never have enough of these. I begin to believe this. Slowly my need to acquire "things" crowds out my need to share. "How can you expect me to make charitable donations? I have too many obligations to take care of already."

I cannot serve both God and mammon. (Matthew 6:24). Whom do I love more?

> "Father God, I pray…
> In my humanness, I seek the good things of life.
> I'm easily convinced that I 'need' something.
> After all, didn't I earn this money myself?
> Why shouldn't I spend it as I wish?
> I merely seek a simple pleasure for myself or my family.
> I often forget that everything I have is a gift from You.
> Help me to keep my priorities straight.
> Teach me that giving is more important than getting.
> Don't let me catch the present plague of 'affluenza.'"

Taking a Walk

Most of my walking exercise is now done on a treadmill. It's convenient, safe, and better during inclement weather. When the beautiful Oregon summers arrive, I often take a walk around the neighborhood, enjoying the fresh air and sun while watching the change taking place near where I live. The outdoor walk also offers a nice change of pace from my daily treadmill routine.

My exercise regime is not always enjoyable. *Far from it.* There are lots of days I moan and groan as I complete my two-mile walk. It's hot, I'm sweaty, and my legs ache. Why do I keep doing this? At my age, one would think I could back off a little bit. But, deep down I know this daily habit is good for me and helps to promote a healthy lifestyle. It's an investment in my overall "quality of life."

We are created in God's image. He has gifted me with this incredibly complex human body. It is my obligation to preserve this *Temple of the Holy Spirit*. Am I doing the best job I can to honor God's gift to me?

> "Father God, I pray...
> In my youth I was lithe and lean,
> Strong and fast and supple.
> Now I am fat and sagging, aching, arthritic...and slow-moving.
> Even as I age help me to appreciate Your miraculous gift of my body.
> Give me the grace to take care of it."

My Priest Friends

As a young boy I looked up to my parish priests. To a youngster, they seemed to be men of great holiness and learning. They taught me to be an altar boy, including all the Latin required. Throughout my growing up years, I was always around priests. I attended a Jesuit university, where I was surrounded by priests daily. I didn't like every priest I knew, but each of them had my utmost respect. Never once in my life did I feel unsafe in the company of a priest.

As an adult my active involvement with our parishes introduced me to many other priests. I knew I was getting old when the parish priest was younger than I. I came to a totally new understanding about what it meant to be priest. These men were trained in theological, liturgical, and pastoral skills, to be sure. But they were just men. Each one I knew had strengths, weaknesses, talents, and shortcomings—just like the rest of us. Some were lonely, others were angry at their bishop, a few were confused about their vocations. To each priest I encountered I offered my complete respect, but I didn't try to get too close. I always attempted to offer the easy friendship of just another guy.

Being a priest is a tough job. Most give a great deal of themselves to God, and we must not expect more of them than He does. Instead, let's be grateful for their service and pray for all priests daily.

> "Father God, I pray.
> Most priests go home to an empty house each day.
> Loneliness sets in after the last Mass on Sunday.
> We want them… right now…when we're sick or dying.
> We expect them to be lawyers, CPAs, and engineers.
> We demand uplifting liturgies, inspiring homilies.
> They must be wise, empathetic, holy, and above reproach.
> But they are just humans…our brothers, sons, and neighbors.
> Lord, teach me to treat all priests with love and understanding."

My Business Career

I have had an interesting career in business that was also financially rewarding. Oh, yes, there were lots of ups and downs—but few people could match the diversity of opportunity that came my way. IBM, Computer Sciences of Australia, fourteen different companies that my partners and I owned and operated, a mini-career in public speaking, 110 consulting clients in the Pacific Northwest, a member of several Boards of Directors, an adjunct professor and lecturer at prestigious universities, a published author.... I was truly blessed with wide-ranging responsibilities and challenges.

"Never a dull moment," as the saying goes. There were moments of euphoria, though. And there were times of great stress verging on panic. Mostly it was a lot of fun.

What life-lessons did I learn from my business involvement? First, I tried to make each decision based on the highest ethical standards. That was "good business practice" and always the right thing to do. Second, I treated every employee with respect and compensated them fairly. Third, I never cut corners on quality or service. My customers rewarded me with continued business. Finally, I always tried to be a good steward of the resources entrusted to me.

Most importantly, I learned that God loaned me whatever skills I have. I often forgot or ignored this basis of my successes. I know now that it underscored everything.

> *"Father God, I pray.*
> *Jesus told us the Parable of the Talents, (Matthew 25: 14-30).*
> *The master rewarded the servant who invested prudently.*
> *Help all business people understand their role as stewards.*
> *Show them how to wisely use and invest their resources.*
> *Hone their skills so they may seek to excel in what is good.*
> *Teach them to reject what is selfish and unfair in business.*
> *Thank you, Lord, for letting me participate in the commerce of this nation.*
> *May You receive Your talents back with interest!"*

Halloween

Actually, I don't like Halloween very much. I resent filling the house with candy and getting up and down all evening long to answer the doorbell. I admit I enjoy seeing the little children all dressed up in their cute costumes. I do find myself short-tempered later in the evening when the scruffy teenagers start showing up. "Why aren't you home studying?" I often grumble. For the last couple of years, my wife and I have turned out all the lights, locked the house, and gone to a restaurant for a leisurely meal. We retreat from the hassle.

There is a lesson one can learn from Halloween, though. Not only do the kids dress up, but many adults don elaborate costumes and attend festive parties. A lot of people find great comfort hiding behind a mask that keeps their real identity a secret. For some, the anonymity emboldens their social intercourse with others. I'm often like that, too. I am reluctant to show my true self to others. I surround myself with layers of protection so no one can really see my imperfections. I guess I would prefer that others see what I want them to see, not the real me.

Some might not like me as much if they saw behind my masks, I think. Maybe this year I'll get the courage to remove my mask and let others see the real me.

"Father God, I pray.
I am afraid to show You who I really am.
Yes, I even hide from You, Lord, who knows all things.
I put out of my mind that Judgment Day is close by.
There I shall stand in front of You, shivering and naked.
I will be forced to rely on Your infinite mercy.
Help me now to be more transparent toward You;
And, to my family, neighbors, and friends."

In the Solitude of a Church

When I enter church on Sunday morning there are always people to greet and quick conversations to hold. Before Mass, there is a hum as people quietly chat with friends, sharing news of the past week. Yes, we are in sacred space, but I like this fellowship aspect of our religion, too. It's easy to feel like a member of the Body of Christ when I worship together with friends and neighbors.

Occasionally I visit the church during the week on some kind of errand. There, by myself, the Presence of God takes on a whole new meaning for me. In this silence, I will often sit in a pew and try to hear what God may be saying to me. The nave, bathed in sunlight and shadows, looks entirely different than it did last Sunday. God is still present, but now I am with Him, alone. In this quiet, He is somehow easier for me to hear. But even when I listen hard I'm not exactly sure what message has been given.

In a world filled with noise, I seek a place where I can be quiet. Each day I must retreat to this space, wherever I may find it. In the silence I will find God. He is there waiting for me, waiting to speak to me. It's a silence I can feel and understand.

> *"Father God, I pray…*
> *I know that I can find You everywhere if I look hard enough.*
> *Crowded markets and teeming roadways are Your home.*
> *Even Sunday worship is a din of voices, song, and prayer.*
> *But I hear You most clearly when I am in our silent place.*
> *Help me to retreat into this quietude each day.*
> *Let me hear Your voice, directing and leading my actions.*
> *Remind me that I have two ears, but only one voice.*
> *Show me how to listen twice as much as I talk."*

They're Always Your Children

As I grow into old age I am acutely aware of how different each of my six children is from one another—cut from the same bolt of cloth, apples fallen from the same tree, but totally unique in talents, disposition, temperament, ambition, philosophy, and outlook on life. At this writing they range in age from their late thirties to mid-forties so they can't be described as "kids" anymore. But no matter how old they become, my wife and I know them as "our children." Even though they are all doing well in life, we still worry about them. *Will their marriages stay healthy? Are their jobs secure? Are their children all on the right path? Do they subscribe to moral and ethical values? Is there a place in their hearts and homes for You, Father God?*

Many of our friends are quietly resigned about the lives their adult children are leading. Conscientiously raised in homes filled with faith in God, some of the children have turned away from the religion of their youth. People ask, "Where did we go wrong? Why didn't our faith stick with our children?"

As Kahil Gibran has written, "God has no grandchildren." We are God's children, and now so are our children. We did our best when they were young. Now it is up to God to take care of them and, as He has promised, to continually draw them to Himself. (Matthew 19: 14)

"Father God, I pray...
Please keep my children safe. Look out for them.
I don't ask that You protect them from all suffering and pain.
This is part of life's journey that we all must bear.
I do ask one favor, Father God.
At the proper moment in their lives, touch them gently.
Send your Spirit to open their minds and hearts to Your love.
Be there for them when I cannot be there.
I turn them over to You."

The Personal Computer

I went to work for the IBM Company in 1956 after completing college. In those days automated accounting was done with punch cards and mechanical sorters, calculators, and printers. A few years later the first wave of commercial computers was introduced. Even the founder of IBM, Thomas Watson, Sr., could not visualize how more than a handful of large computers would ever be needed. These huge electronic machines were relatively powerful, but that had nothing like the computing capacity of today's ubiquitous personal computer. My small desk top computer is hundreds of times more flexible and powerful than the computers I sold as a young salesman.

For many of us—*not all*—computers have become central to our daily activities. *Where would I be without email, word processing, access to the Internet, my investment and medical records, and so much more?* A hard drive crash or a nasty virus that shuts me down will quickly reveal how dependent I am on my computer. Personal computing has a dark side, too. "Surfing the net" has become addictive for many. Pornographic material is rampant and easily accessed. "Chat rooms" lure innocents who are preyed upon by monsters. Sites promoting hate and bigotry are everywhere.

I must strive to use my personal computer to promote good and curtail evil.

"Father God, I pray…
I marvel at the tremendous technology sitting on my desk.
At my fingertips I have a world full of information.
I can write and compute with ease and accuracy.
Communication with people continents away is simple.
Is all this done 'for the greater glory of God?' No.
Show me how to use this electronic power to change the world.
Let me see Your hand in my daily computer activity."

Serving in the Military

I was commissioned a Second Lieutenant upon graduation from college. I thought I was pretty hot stuff—an "officer and a gentleman"—things like that. When I was ordered to active duty with the Army my civilian boss said: "The two years will probably do you good." He was right. I spent my time at Ft. Bliss, TX. It was a worthwhile experience. I returned home more mature, disciplined, and with a valuable new set of skills. I continued my service with the National Guard and Army Reserve for an additional five years. I was honorably discharged with the rank of Captain.

The two years on active duty involved hard work and exposed me to difficult situations. My maturity involved learning that I was not the one in control. The discipline forced me to see that I couldn't skate through life. Thanks be to God, I was never forced to test my mettle in combat.

Virtues learned in the Army carried over to my life. I began developing a basic maturity about God being in control of things. Discipline required that I lead a moral life on a continual basis.

Many years later, I'm still trying to apply these lessons.

"Father God, I pray.
The soldier is often lionized as a hero bigger than life.
Bravely, he or she patrols dangerous places,
There is always contact with fellow soldiers right and left.
Reaction to the enemy is based on rigorous training.
Lord, is this another metaphor for my life?
I often find myself in dangerous places.
I rely on my neighbors to help me through hard places.
My reaction to evil is based on Your grace and aid.
Help me to lead a Christian life as Your soldier, serving well."

Preparing for Winter

The chill winds and showery days of late autumn remind me that I must get busy preparing the house for winter. Furnace filters need replacing. The garden hoses are emptied of water and rolled up for storage. The foundation vents must be plugged with their Styrofoam blocks. Outside hose bibs are drained and protective covers are installed. Gutters are cleared of debris and leaves. The yard sprinkler system is emptied and turned off. All in all, there are lots of chores one must complete before winter arrives.

This is much the same for those of us in the autumn of our lives. I hope my current state of productive activity and relative good health will continue indefinitely—but I know it won't. It is time for me to prepare physically, emotionally, and spiritually for what is just around the corner. *Do I have open accounts with friends or family? Are there hurts that must be reconciled? Am I prudently caring for my physical wellbeing? Do I ask God for a sense of trust in His overall plan for my life? Am I prepared for Judgment Day?*

"You know neither the day nor the hour." (Matthew 24: 36). *Help me treat each new dawning as if it will be my last here on earth.*

> "Father God, I pray…
> Time drones on inexorably.
> Each tick of the clock records another bygone moment
> There is less sand in the hourglass every day.
> Teach me to count the time left to me as opportunity.
> Show me how to love more, reconcile more, trust more.
> By Your grace, Lord, I will live each day to the fullest.
> When I meet You face to face on Judgment Day,
> I hope You say, 'Well done, good and faithful servant.'"

Guests for Dinner

I feel a pleasant anticipation when we have guests invited to dinner. Well in advance, I like to cover the dining room table with a nice tablecloth, set the table using our "special" dishes, and even put out crystal goblets for water. As it gets close to arrival time, I will double check that everything is prepared, including pre-dinner snacks and drinks. I am satisfied if everything appears to be in order. Perhaps I'm hoping our guests will notice the care and attention that has gone into getting ready for their visit to our home.

Hospitality should not be confined to having guests for dinner. On a daily basis I have the opportunity to do things for others that lets them feel my interest and concern. A friendly wave to the mailperson. A smile for the checker at the grocery store. A visit to a friend in the hospital. Listening intently to someone tell the story of a wounded marriage, an ominous illness, or a shattering job loss. All these things are acts of hospitality. They witness to a sense of opening my arms and heart to others who enter my human space.

Unfortunately I sometimes miss these opportunities because of a sour mood, my selfishness, or sullen disinterest. I need to work on being hospitable to everyone I meet, not just some people—and not just at times of *my* choosing.

> "Father God, I pray…
> I sometimes feel like the Levite in the Gospel story.
> He passed by the man wounded by robbers.
> It wasn't convenient to stop and help a fellow human.
> I often pick and choose the time I offer hospitality.
> It's easy when I am with friends who like me.
> But strangers need my hospitality, too.
> Dear God, give me the grace to always care for others.
> Teach me to be welcoming to everyone I meet."

Death of an Old Friend

Art and I knew each other for about thirty years. We went to the same church; his son attended high school with my boys and we both coached youth baseball teams. Art loved to golf and in his later years became a PGA golf official. You wouldn't call us "buddies" joined at the hip, but we saw one another often. Over the years we developed a pleasant friendship and enjoyed each other's company. If I'd faced a crisis, I could have called on Art. I knew he would have responded by doing everything possible for me.

After we moved from California to Oregon, we didn't see Art as often. Whenever we visited our old home area, Art and his wife, Donna, were on our list of "must see" people. Even the thousand-mile distance didn't dampen our continuing friendship. Late one October, we got an invitation to attend Art's seventieth birthday party in mid-November. About a week before the party, Art arose early, as usual, sat in his recliner chair with a morning cup of coffee and died. A blood clot broke loose somewhere and stopped his heart.

Those losses are tough to take. Even though I have complete faith in the Resurrection, my human nature is wounded by a friend's death. *How do I keep these events in the proper perspective?*

> "Father God, I pray.
> I feel sad when friends and loved ones die.
> Almost selfishly, I want to hold on to their presence.
> It pleases me when I can enjoy their company.
> But then they're gone, and this leaves me feeling empty.
> Accepting Your plan for each of our lives is hard.
> I want things organized and accomplished by my plan, not Yours.
> Teach me to be willingly, cheerfully accepting.
> Show me Your loving hand in my life and in other's lives, too."

Pain

All human beings suffer pain at one time or another. Who knows what type of pain hurts the most: physical pain, emotional pain, or spiritual pain? Is there one of us who would *embrace* pain? I don't like pain one bit. I've been lucky in my life. I have probably experienced less physical pain than most people. Only in recent years have medical conditions and an aging body produced some chronic pain. Still, I'm sure it is nothing compared to what others must face routinely.

Emotional and spiritual pain may be even more searing. I know some parents of drug-addicted kids, women psychologically abused by their spouses, and spiritually lost people. Their pain must be excruciating. Whenever I think of pain, I need only reflect on the passion and death of Jesus Christ. God, truly human, endured the most exquisite of all suffering. Remarkably, it was suffered because He loved me. It is unspeakable to contemplate.

What am I to think about my own personal pain? *Embrace it?* No, of course not! Am I to accept it as part of the human condition and the cycle of life? This I must do. I can't avoid it. I must try to make it meaningful and effective on some level. *Can I offer my minor little pain as a prayer for someone who needs courage and strength? How else can I accept the inevitability of pain in my life?*

"I don't like it, Lord, but help me to bear my pain with grace."

> *"Father God, I pray…*
> *You exhort us to take up our cross daily and follow You.*
> *I agree to do so reluctantly and conditionally.*
> *I'll carry my cross, Lord, but please make it light.*
> *Let the others bear cancer, AIDS, MS, Parkinson's.*
> *But not me. I am too afraid of the pain You might send me.*
> *What I really need is courage, grace, and acceptance.*
> *Will you send me the strength I need?*
> *Will you make a hero out of a coward?"*

Neighbors

We lived in one house in Southern California for twenty-six years. We have lived for fourteen years in one house in Oregon. In both places we were blessed with wonderful neighbors. June and Steve lived across the street in Fullerton, CA. They became like family to us. My wife called June her "sister." Our kids referred to them as "Grandma June" and "Grandpa Steve." Steve was a natural handyman (I'm not) and was always helping me fix something around our house. They were about fifteen years older than we were. It was very sad for us to watch them age, become frail, and eventually pass away. We loved them dearly.

Jeff and Penni are our next-door neighbors in Tualatin. They are about twenty years younger than we are. Jeff is a hardworking guy and Penni is always busy with creative projects. They are devoted to their two college-age children. They are also extremely caring and helpful to us. Jeff often brings the morning newspaper to our door. He has even shoveled our sidewalk when snow has fallen.

It is very easy to love neighbors who seem to love you back. But what of the neighbors who aren't so appealing? We've had a few we frankly didn't like because we felt they were poor neighbors.

Did God tell me that I could love just some of my neighbors?

"Father God, I pray.
I must love God with all my heart.
I must love my neighbor as myself.
This is the essence of the Christian life. Jesus said so.
From a human perspective, I don't like all my neighbors.
Not in the neighborhood, not in the country, not in the world.
You love them all unconditionally, Lord;
Why can't I?
Help me, God, in my weakness to do better at loving."

A Restaurant Dinner

For many years my wife and I have gone out to dinner at least once a week. We rotate among our favorite places and enjoy a variety of ethnic foods, seafood, and American cuisine. I especially like the Mexican restaurants because I can practice my halting Spanish on the waiters. They are usually good-humored and patient, although I have seen some of them shaking their heads as they left the table after taking our order.

Even with places we know, sometimes the food served is different from what we expected. Maybe the vegetables are overcooked. Perhaps the serving size is too large. Sometimes the food just doesn't taste like we prepare it at home. Unless it's really bad, we seldom grumble. We just accept what is served but tuck away in our memories that we won't order *that* again.

I find a disappointing restaurant meal can be a lesson for my daily life. Sometimes I am presented with some incident I don't like, or that is unexpected. I find I have two choices: complain, or accept things as they are. I'm not as patient with daily events as I am in a restaurant. When things in my life don't turn out as I wish, I find it easy to show my anger or frustration with what has happened.

Maybe I should learn to be more patient and understanding.

"Father God, I pray…
Too often, I cry out, 'Life isn't fair.'
I want You to deal me a hand full of aces and kings.
Send the debilitating illness or nagging pain to someone else.
Save the daily difficulties in life for others, not me.
I like my pathways to be straight and smooth.
I don't like it when You send me disruptive trouble.
Does that make me selfish, soft, and self-absorbed?
Help me to be more accepting of what comes my way."

Washing the Car

I've always tried to maintain my vehicles well. That includes keeping the interior vacuumed and exterior washed and polished. In my younger days I did all this myself. Now I take a trip to the local car wash and pay to have this job completed by others. The car always looks sharp when it exits the wash tunnel. On the way home it seems inevitable that I will encounter a puddle or drive through a muddy stretch. By the time the car is back in my garage, it is already starting to look grimy. So, it's back to the car wash in a few days to start over again. And again. And again.

Stop and think about all the things in life you have to do again in a few minutes, days, weeks, or months. Brushing teeth. Going to the bathroom. Washing hands. Preparing food. Sleeping. Making the bed. Cleaning the house. Most of us would be hard pressed to name a handful of things that, once completed, would never have to be done again. Most of our activities we do *again and again and again*.

This is not a bad thing. Most of our lives have a routine and a rhythm that provide us with stability, order, and predictability. I need to apply this to my prayer life, too. I need to be in touch with God. *Over and over and over*. Again and again and again.

I must work to keep my prayer stable, rhythmic, and routine.

"Father God, I pray…
I find time for a hundred things that must be done each day.
Washing, cleaning, cooking, exercising will be completed.
But sometimes I forget You in my daily routine.
Consumed with mundane chores, I often ignore Your call.
You patiently wait for me to respond to Your love.
I turn to You when it suits me, when I need Your help.
Teach me, Lord, that my prayer life must be consistent, routine, and rhythmic.
Over and over and over. Again and again and again."

Christmas Lights

As Christmas approaches I decorate the bushes in our front yard with lights. I used to have more elaborate lighting, but I'm no longer comfortable climbing ladders, so I stick to lighting the low shrubs. From the street, everything still looks attractive, so I am usually satisfied with my work.

I do have one complaint, though. I have neighbors who begin putting up extensive lighting decorations on the day after Thanksgiving. I'm not unhappy with the way their houses look once the task is completed—they're beautiful. But I wonder why they have to get started *so soon*. As a boy, I remember the First Sunday of Advent. This was the time to begin preparation for the coming of baby Jesus one month away. We used to put up our tree on Christmas Eve. It signaled that the waiting was just about over and the Feast of the Incarnation was here. Maybe I'm just clinging to past traditions.

But I'm going to stick to my guns. Instead of rushing directly to the Christmas celebration, I will keep the tradition of quiet waiting and anticipation. My house will continue to be a dark island in a sea of lights until just a few days before Christmas. The wait is worth it.

On Christmas Day, "O Come, O Come, Emmanuel" will be fulfilled! Alleluia! My God has taken the form of a man!

"Father God, I pray…
Like the expectant woman, I quietly await a new birth.
Not just any birth, but the Son of God made man.
My weak intellect is overwhelmed by this gift to us.
How could He love us…me…so much?
I feel called to prepare my soul for this stupendous gift.
What can I possibly do to show my appreciation?
My incarnated Lord says, 'Respond to Me as best you can.'"

A Visit from Grandchildren

Presently we have fourteen grandchildren. Except for the two that live nearby, the rest are scattered around the country. Other than our annual family reunion, we don't get to see too many of the kids very often. I'm pretty sure that is not a good thing for my wife or me.

When we do get visits, it is quite an experience for us. First, the children are eager to do and see things that are different from their home environments. Because there are many attractions in our region, it is usually pretty easy to keep the kids occupied. There is a price to pay for this busyness. My wife and I find we are exhausted at the end of a day-long outing, while the kids are still full of energy and looking forward to the next adventure tomorrow. *What happened to the stamina and enthusiasm of our younger days?* Obviously, it is gone.

Second, we love the quiet moments around the dinner table. We look into the little faces and trusting eyes as they tell their stories about school, their friends, their sporting activities. Their sincerity and openness is most engaging. We treasure these conversations.

Most of all these visits remind me of the cycle of life and death. I am a link to the past for these little children. They are my link to immortality. God's plan for each stage of our lives seems so simple, yet perfect. I must savor each part of my life, not battle against it.

> *"Father God, I pray…*
> *You have blessed me with children and grandchildren.*
> *Each one possesses a unique personality and spirit.*
> *They are young and view the future with hope and enthusiasm.*
> *My aging body reminds me that my earthly life now grows short.*
> *Let them teach me about trust and love and optimism.*
> *Let me teach them about fortitude and integrity and faith.*
> *May I experience the future while in their presence;*
> *May they experience their family history in my presence."*

On Being a Eucharistic Minister

One of the most profound honors given a Catholic lay person is an invitation to be a Eucharistic minister. It doesn't imply that you are holier, more reverent, or a "better" Catholic than anybody else. It does mean that you have been entrusted with the awesome task of giving the Body and Blood of Jesus Christ to your fellow parishioners during Mass. I believe that *how* I perform my duties influences what kind of encounter each person has with Jesus.

Most Catholics have experienced the perfunctory distribution of Holy Communion by priest and lay minister alike. There is no smile or eye contact; they look past you to the next person in line. The sacred bread is quickly placed on your palm. One feels an unspoken "Move on—there are more in line." I do not judge here. But I feel called to a different level of contact with each person. As every individual approaches, I remind myself: *Take your time. Smile. Make serious eye contact. Touch his or her hand and linger there as you slowly, reverently place the host on the palm.* Young and old, male and female, must all experience the same meaningful exchange with me.

I have been blessed with this stewardship of handling the Lord's Body and Blood. I try to do this small work well so that I might serve Christ well and be called to even larger tasks of building up God's Kingdom here on earth.

> "Father God, I pray…
> You clearly know my many shortcomings.
> Lord, I am not worthy to receive You.
> I also feel inadequate giving You to others.
> But, I have been called and I humbly accept this ministry.
> Let each recipient of Communion see Your face in mine;
> Feel Your touch in my touch; see Your smile in mine.
> Help me to never lose my reverence for the Eucharist.
> 'Say but the word and my soul (and theirs) shall be healed.'"

Wrapping a Present

As a young boy I was taught that I must be very careful about wrapping a gift to give to someone. A careless or slipshod job meant that I was too lazy or self-absorbed to show my care and affection for the recipient of the gift. "Carefully cut the paper to have enough, but not too much, to cover the gift," I was told. "Turn the box or package over so the paper seam will be on the bottom. Make sure that the excess paper is equal at each end. Fold the ends over neatly and use just enough tape to seal the package."

Adding ribbon or bows was done with equal care. No matter how long it took, I was told that I should prepare each wrapped gift as neatly as I could.

The same care should apply in my conversations, I decided. I should wrap my words very carefully, making sure that nothing I say gives the impression I really don't care. By avoiding needless or hurtful words, my discussions with others can show the respect and love I have for the other person. I know from experience that harsh words can cause a lot of pain. How many of us can recall a destructive conversation with a spouse, a child, a family member, friend or neighbor? We may still say to ourselves, *If only I hadn't said those words.*

I must remember always to wrap my words carefully in a bright package made up of gentleness, kindness, truth, and love—ready for delivery.

> "Father God, I pray…
> Too often, I catch myself blurting out hurtful words to others.
> Words, I know, can bite, sting, and wound.
> I often use words like a rapier to pierce others through.
> Why can't I learn to always speak sweetly and lovingly?
> What causes me to gain advantage with an acid vocabulary?
> I hate it when others do this to me. How must they feel?
> Lord, I need Your help to curb my tongue sometimes.
> Let me always speak from a meek and gentle heart."

Watching Television

We're probably not your average TV-watching family. We never watch the prime time "sitcoms" shown on the big networks. We tune in the cable networks like *ESPN, The History Channel, Fox News,* and *Arts & Entertainment*. Occasionally we get "hooked" on one of the police and science dramas like *NYPD Blue* or *CSI*. As far as programs like *Seinfeld, Friends,* and the reality shows—never saw one single episode and don't feel we missed a thing.

Television can entertain, inform, hypnotize, and mindlessly waste time. I'm probably better off reading a book, writing a letter, or talking to my wife. When I see the relentless news stories of all manner of tragedies I feel agitated, distressed, and helpless. These and the political shows where two ideologues scream over each other cause me to hit the "mute" button on the remote control. I can shut out the noise and silence what I do not like or want to hear.

Television is a window on the world. *Mute* allows me to selectively ignore the stories I do not wish to hear. My eyes are also a window on the world I live in. I cannot use a remote control to shut out injustices observed, harsh words spoken, psychic wounds inflicted, and hate spewed out from one person on another. No, I cannot turn my back on the evil that I see in my little world. I must respond to it. God says so.

> "Father God, I pray.
> When I see bad things happening, I'm supposed to respond.
> But how, Lord? I don't know what to do.
> I don't want to get involved or look like a 'do-gooder.'
> 'Just ignore it and it will go away,' I tell myself.
> 'Perhaps no one will know that I profess to be a Christian.'
> It doesn't work that way, does it, Father God?
> Loving my neighbor means I must stand up for him, too."

Cooking

When I told my wife I was retiring she said she wanted to retire, too. To her, that meant she would be relieved of the cooking chores after forty-plus years preparing food for our kids and me. I do most of the cooking now. I'm not passionate about it and usually I stick to pretty easy things, but it is a labor of love. I figure she did her stint so the least I can do is give her relief now. She tells me my food is wonderful. I think any food she doesn't have to cook is probably delicious to her. Still, I don't mind the compliments.

I do enjoy planning and preparing meals for guests. I leaf through cookbooks and recipe files searching for things that are a little different, don't require lots of preparation time, and promise to please everyone's palates. I get a little uptight at mealtime. I worry about the timing of having everything done concurrently. It's fun when the women guests say appreciatively, "Did you prepare this yourself?" I also enjoy the sour looks from the men who think I'm raising the bar too high for them in their *own* households.

Preparing food for others nourishes their bodies. I think I am also called to nourish the spirits and souls of those I encounter each day. God asks me to provide a different kind of spiritual sustenance to others whether they are family members, guests, neighbors, or strangers. By my words, actions, and attitudes, I can uplift those I meet daily. *Who knows?* That may be even more important than bodily food to some people…on certain days.

> "Father God, I pray…
> Tasty food pleases our mouths and warms our stomachs.
> Important events are often celebrated with meals.
> I pray that You bless those who prepare food for others.
> Let them always do their work with love for those they feed.
> Help me, Lord, to also nourish souls and spirits.
> My gentle, kind words may mean more than earthly food."

An Argument with a Friend

It started out pleasant enough—a discussion between friends over lunch. We began talking about our wives' current projects, switched to discussing the latest movies, and then moved to articles in the local newspaper. Somehow this led to the current political contest. My friend and I share common views about many things, but politics is not one of them. We were respectful at first. Both of us commented without interruption. As the discussion continued, our demeanors changed, however. There was less cordial give-and-take, more acrimony in our voices. Finally we resorted to insulting comments about the other's opinions and lack of insight. We had reached a stony impasse. The conversation concluded in icy silence.

How stupid of me! It is pathetic that I would wound a friendship over something as transitory as politics. It was not necessary for me to abandon my principles. I should have seen that this topic was leading to someplace bad. I needed to change the subject as soon as I sensed our ideas were in concrete and 180° apart on this issue.

I'm afraid this happens to me too often. Perhaps my thinking has become rigid and I no longer listen to the views of others. *Is it pride? Is it self-righteousness? Have I become a know-it-all who arrogantly proclaims intellectual superiority over my friends?* Whatever, I need God's help to initiate reconciliation with my friend.

> "Father God, I pray…
> I form my ideas until I achieve a comfortable position.
> My ideas are well thought out and carefully reasoned.
> Having taken this effort, how could I possibly be wrong?
> 'I bristle when you challenge me; you confront my logic.
> You must be wrong, friend. My reasoning is solid.'
> Lord, forcefully show me how ridiculous I have become.
> Help me learn from others.
> Help me reconcile with friends I have carelessly wounded."

Home Repairs

Here is a good lesson for a homeowner: don't put off needed repairs. Everyone who owns a home knows that things go wrong once in a while. Fuses blow, faucets drip, roofs leak, cement cracks, paint fades. The list can seem endless, especially if you're living in an older home.

I may be the world's worst handyman or do-it-yourself guy, but I am quick to see when things need fixing. Others complete these chores themselves. My lack of skills often requires me to hire someone to solve my problem. Either way, the repair must be done. Little problems left untended seem to become big problems later on.

There's another lesson here. Patching up your home is like mending relations with family and friends when something has become broken. The thoughtless word, the unintentional slight, taking a loved one for granted—all these things need immediate repair. Like the home repairs left for later, slightly broken relationships can turn out to be big problems if not addressed right now.

It's hard for me to take the first step. Pride and ego get in the way. I rationalize that the problem wasn't really my fault. *Let them come and apologize to me*, I think. I know this is the wrong approach. Relationships are not 50/50 percent propositions. All successful relationships are 75/75 percent. I must take the first step to set things right. Even when it is hard to do. I must reach out to others.

> "Father God, I pray…
> Little hurts and offenses happen so easily.
> A careless comment, a cruel response can wound.
> Small breaks in a relationship must be fixed immediately.
> Why am I reluctant to be the first to apologize?
> I need to the first one to patch things up.
> Even when it is hard, Lord, help me to initiate healing.
> 'To whom I have given much, much will be expected.'" (Mark 4: 25)

A New Pastor

Next July our parish is due to get a new pastor. Father Dick has been here for twelve years, and that's the limit for a priest's stay in one place. I suppose there are some exceptions but they won't apply in our case.

Over that long a time we can get pretty comfortable with a parish priest. I guess he can get equally used to the parish and its people. In theory, I think it's a good idea to move the priests around on some regular basis. I just don't like it when it happens to me and my parish. At the beginning of an assignment, both people and priest have idealized expectations. The parish visualizes a dynamic, hard-charging leader who will be charming, a pious liturgist, and an inspirational homilist. The priest may think he is getting a fresh start with folks who will be understanding, not too demanding, and willing to share the administrative and financial burden of running the parish. Neither side ever gets all that is hoped for. The priest turns out to be a guy with strengths and weaknesses who is doing his best to fulfill his vocation. The people turn out to be the same ones he left behind in his old parish. Some are friendly and helpful, others are relentlessly critical, and the majority provide little support with time, talent, or treasure. In short, the parish turns out to be another human organization with all *that* implies, both good and bad.

I hate to see an old friend depart. I have trepidation about the new pastor. What if things just don't work out? I will find out soon.

> "Father God, I pray…
> I don't like change. It disrupts the rhythm of my routine.
> I am comfortable in the relationship with my priest.
> He clearly knows my weaknesses and strengths.
> He is now called to shepherd a different group.
> I must adjust to the personality of a new pastor.
> This is hard for me, Lord. Help me to accept new ideas.
> Condition my soul for the changes that will surely come."

The Sunday Collection

For reasons unknown to me Catholics are not very generous when contributing to their Church. There are obvious exceptions; many give *substantial* amounts. On average, however, we Catholics give a much lower percentage of our incomes than most Protestants do. Even in affluent parishes about one-fifth of the registered families provide almost 80 percent of the ordinary income. Those who regularly use giving envelopes always contribute the great bulk of the money. The "loose plate" of bills and coins is usually insignificant.

I find this to be very discouraging. How can we convince our fellow religionists that faithful stewardship is important? Everything we have—*everything*—is a gift from God. We might like to think that the money we earn and the wealth we have accumulated is due to our efforts. It is not. Only by the grace of God do we earn our daily bread.

I used to help count the collection. I won't do that anymore. I found myself being judgmental of others as I recorded the gifts. "They could give more," I would say silently. That wasn't good for my soul. My judgment was probably wrong, anyway; how would I know about any family's personal situation?

Stewardship is between God and me. I must never judge others.

"Father God, I pray…
Our churches do not survive on air.
There are bills to pay, people to hire, and services to fund.
Heating, cooling, repairs, power, books, candles, and incense.
Human needs and spiritual needs must all be funded.
Yet I am reluctant to contribute much of my money.
I know I should give God what is right.
Too often, I only offer Him what is left.
Help me to understand that what I have is a gift from You."

The Perfect Day

When we lived in Southern California we experienced a lot of nice days. After moving to Oregon we have fewer nice days. But we have had some *perfect* days. You know what I mean...absolutely crystal clear skies, temperature around seventy-two degrees, a gentle breeze blowing, and just a few puffy clouds in the sky. Those days are glorious and make you feel good just to be alive. They make up for any gray and rainy days we must endure.

I just seem to experience all of nature more fully on a perfect day. The sky is *so blue!* The temperature is just right; not too warm, not too cool. Even if I'm walking briskly the slight breeze keeps me comfortable. I can glance to the east and see snow-covered Mt. Hood. To the northeast, I spot Mt. St. Helens. The towering fir trees in my neighborhood and on the distant hills cast inviting shadows. *How could anyone deny there is a God in the face of this incredible beauty and majesty?*

I am not generally an "outdoorsy person." I have little interest in hiking through the woods, camping in remote areas, climbing the local mountains, or fishing in the nearby wild streams. A hot shower, a comfortable hotel bed, and a five-star meal are more to my liking. Even with this urban orientation I see the hand of my Creator very clearly, especially on a perfect day.

"My God, help me to see You even on stormy days, too."

"Father God, I pray…
Some people ask: How do we know that God exists?
We cannot see Him; show us some proof!
I tell them to walk through the Redwood forests in California.
Stand on the ocean shore as the sun sets in the West.
Put your index finger into the hand of a newborn baby.
Stand on the rim and look into the blue of Crater Lake.
O God! Your creation is majestic and awesome."

On Being Fired

I have been fired from three jobs. The first time was humiliating. The second time was unjust. The third time was a tremendous blessing. Being terminated can leave a deep, ugly wound on your spirit. The first time, my employer's company was acquired. After the merger a meeting was called. It was announced in front of my peers that I would be replaced with someone new. I was crushed and deeply embarrassed.

Later I was managing a small company with limited capital. My normal work schedule was a sixteen–to–eighteen–hour–day, six days per week. Hard work was beginning to pay off. I asked the owner for additional resources so that I could capitalize on our success. He scoffed at me. "You should have gotten the job done with what you had," he said, then fired me on the spot. Finally, I sold a company I was managing. After a year the new owner said he wanted to bring in someone new. I was relieved! Now I could actually retire and begin following other goals and dreams.

Being fired is one human way of understanding the humiliation of crucifixion. It is a painful and agonizing experience, leading ultimately to abject hopelessness and excruciating death. The end of the journey is the tomb. Some may find "resurrection" in a fulfilling new job. Others may be permanently scarred and never find meaningful employment again.

I must be compassionate to those who have lost their jobs.

"Father God, I pray…
New jobs are created, other jobs are ended.
Mere statistics to me; numbers that do not affect me.
But each lost job is more than data in a news report.
A family breadwinner is now without work and income.
Fear and stress rise as savings are depleted.
These people are not mere statistics.
They are members of the Body of Christ.
Their pain and agony must be shared by all.
Teach me to give a helping hand to all without work."

The Greeting Card

I usually love to shop for greeting cards. The exceptions: the days just before Valentine's Day and Mother's Day are too crowded with panicked men trying to find a last minute selection. Most times it is enjoyable to look through cards. Some are really funny. It's a hoot to watch someone burst out laughing while reviewing the possibilities. Cards are available in a variety of styles: serious, endearing, romantic, hilarious, and even risqué. I often wonder where they find the people who compose the printed sentiments. You would think there were only so many ways to say, "I love you, Mom/Wife/Sweetheart," but each time I shop there are new cards with fresh verses inside and out. I'm always looking for just the right words and thoughts to convey my feelings. Given enough time, I find what I am looking for.

I see a parallel between greeting cards and prayer. Many people rely on printed pamphlets or books to provide order to their prayer lives. Like the greeting cards, it's interesting that new material is being printed all the time…like this book. Is there a new way to say, "I love you, God," or "I'm sorry, God," or "Help me, God?" Apparently *yes*, since new material is published daily.

Cards are available that are blank inside. You can write in your own sentiment. Sometimes they suit me best. Prayers can be like that, too. When books and models don't work, make up your own prayers. I think God hears them—perhaps even better than He does the others.

> "Father God, I pray.
> On a human level, my prayers seem so inarticulate.
> I feel like my words are jumbled, confused, unorganized.
> I think You hear them all and understand their meaning.
> But when I am discouraged or feeling my own sinfulness—
> Do You hear me then, too?
> Give me confidence, Lord, that my prayers are heard.
> Let me trust in Your unconditional love for me."

Christmas Gift Shopping

Our family used to have an elaborate Christmas gift exchange program. Everyone was in the mix—our six kids, their spouses, my wife and me. There were lots of rules and the drawing of names in October was complicated. People hated to draw certain names (like mine) that were difficult to shop for. We abandoned the scheme several years ago. Who needed the extra hassle at Christmas time? Life was frantic enough, especially for those with little children.

I bemoan the fact that Christmas has lost any semblance of its true meaning. It is mostly an economic event providing many retailers with close to 75 percent of their yearly sales volume. The Incarnation of the Lord has taken a back seat to this feeding frenzy. Yes, there is some bland sentimentality about "peace on earth and good will toward men," but not much penetrates our frenetic rush to buy presents, attend holiday parties, and prepare feasts for guest and family alike. *Talk about wrong priorities!*

Still, I can find meaning in my gift shopping. Instead of just buying "more stuff," I try hard to find something that expresses my love and care for the recipient. I think that is what Christmas may be all about. How do we truly show others how much we love and care for them? That idea is an imitation of what God did for us by sending His Son.

> "Father God, I pray…
> I am turned off by the excesses I see at Christmastime.
> Bright boxes stacked three-deep under the lighted trees.
> Children rip and tear the wrapping off their presents;
> They hardly see one gift inside before moving on to another.
> How can I set a proper example for my grandchildren?
> Can my actions lead them to experience the Greatest Gift?
> Without spoiling their excitement over a Christmas present, Lord,
> Help me to teach them what a gift God has given to all of us in His Son."

The Garage Attic

We have a pull-down ladder in the ceiling of our garage. It provides access to a storage attic. When we first moved into our home the space was used to store Christmas decorations. As time passed, more and more things were placed in this attic. Now every time I climb the ladder carrying stuff I'm surprised how crowded and cluttered the plywood floor of this dark, cramped room has become. I need to get up there and "clean house." That's hard to do because I always think I'm going to eventually need the junk and trash I have stored there. I rationalize that the first time I dispose of something is when I'll wish I still had it. This idea also conveniently saves me from doing any work.

My soul has an attic, too. When I look carefully, I see a lot of junk, trash, and baggage that I don't want and should have gotten rid of long ago. There's a dusty carton filled with grudges I've held. I see another grimy box filled with bias, prejudice, self-righteousness, and judgment of others. I find a bag loaded with anger, self-pity, and personal doubts. This storage space is badly in need of a spring cleaning but, like the attic in my garage, I delay making a clean sweep of it. Why?

Do I savor renewing old grudges? Is there something perversely pleasurable about resurrecting old hurts or reliving old anger? I know there is a dark, cramped part of my soul that I cannot ignore. *I must ask the Lord to help me rid myself of this negative stuff.*

"Father God, I pray…
Each of us possesses a dark side to our souls.
As I know all too well, I am no exception.
St. Paul gave us a clear explanation for this problem:
'The good I would do, I do not do.
The evil I would avoid, I do.'
To sweep clean these dusty, grimy places is hard work.
I cannot possibly complete this labor without Your help.
Lord, give me the grace to clear out the shadowy attic of my soul."

The Parish Fundraising Committee

Our parish would be hurting financially if it were not for fundraising events. We put on a parish auction, garage sales, spaghetti dinners, and pancake breakfasts—just to name a few. Almost everyone who attends enjoys himself, but in our parish it seems the entire organizing burden falls on a very few people. I'm sure that's true for other churches, as well. The same handful of folks does all the work while the rest of us just show up. That doesn't seem right to me.

I'm sure some people get involved because they enjoy doing the necessary work. It might be a nice diversion for them and, besides, they like the other parishioners they're working with. Most would prefer to be home watching TV or reading a book instead of planning how to feed 350 people spaghetti or figuring out how to recruit people to clean up afterwards. The worst part comes when the event is finally over. How often do you think someone says "thank you" to a volunteer chairperson of a parish event? I'm afraid that is a very rare occurrence.

I pitch in on these committees once in a while. I'm sure it is not often enough. I should have a special appreciation for those who make personal sacrifices in order to conduct smooth-running and enjoyable parish events. Their work must rate a unique positive notation in the mythical book kept by St. Peter at the Pearly Gates.

> "Father God, I pray…
> *Why does parish work fall on such a small handful of people?*
> *Many are happy to write a check giving part of their treasure,*
> *But do not ask them to give the precious commodity of time.*
> *I find myself shirking these volunteer jobs just like others.*
> *'I'm older now…. I'm very busy…. I do other things at church….'*
> *Excuses! I rationalize in order to avoid helping out.*
> *Lord, help me to always see the dignity and sacrifice of church volunteers.*"

Choosing Life

We have a giant societal divide in this country about the question of life: "When does life begin?" "Do I have the right to end my life if I am in exquisite emotional or bodily pain?" "Can the death penalty ever be just?" "Do women have the right to control their own bodies?" "Is an abortion *ever* justified?" Some issues can be rationally and civilly discussed by people of good will. This topic, however, has polarized us as a nation. Any attempt at dialog between the two sides seems to immediately break down into shouting, invective, and rigidity.

I hope my strongly held positions on this issue have been formed by careful review of the available facts. I believe life begins at conception. Abortion is wrong because it takes an innocent life. Our life is a gift from God, so suicide is selfish and arrogant. I am conflicted on the death penalty. Even the Catechism of the Catholic Church is ambiguous about this. I have friends who hold completely opposite positions about life issues. I lack the skill to engage them in conversations about these things, and I worry that our discussions will turn impolite, uncivil, or destructive.

I'm concerned that I have never had to consider abortion or suicide in my own family. *What if my teenage granddaughter had become pregnant and wanted an abortion? How would I have dealt with that? What about a suicide in the family?* I honestly don't know.

"Father God, I pray…
You tell me that I am made in Your image.
My very life is Your benevolent gift to me.
Can I reject this gift through abortion or suicide?
What about the state-sponsored death penalty?
The issue looks black and white to me.
Others say, 'No, you have it all wrong.'
Lord, give me the grace to engage others in gentle debate.
Give me the words that might change their hearts."

Compassion

We often experience compassion for others. Think of September 11, 2001. Almost everyone felt a deep sense of sympathy and pain for the innocent victims of the terrorist actions. Horrible pictures and written accounts personalized the loss so many families suffered. We felt the terror of those in the airplanes. Our flesh crawled watching people jump from buildings. Heroic deaths of firefighters and police were impossible to imagine. Our spirits were scarred by the terrible pain inflicted on the surviving families.

I recall no compassionate expression for the families of the terrorists. *Should I expect that the mothers, fathers, wives, and siblings of the killers felt no pain at the death of their loved one?* No, I believe some Middle Eastern mothers and wives cried bitterly, having lost a son or husband.

Must I feel equal sympathy for victim and perpetrator alike? Am I expected to recognize the pain and alleviate the suffering of the child molester? The serial murderer? The drunk driver who kills a family? The assassinated abortion doctor? What limits *can* I place on my compassion for others?

It is easy to have empathy for those who are like us, who share our values, whose skin is our color, whose worldview match ours. "Are You calling me to extend compassion to all the others, Lord? I cannot do this unless You provide me with monumental grace."

> "Father God, I pray…
> I cry when I see others crying. 'Let me wipe away your tears,'
>   I think.
> It could have been me who suffered that dreadful loss.
> You look, act, and think like me. And so I share your pain.
> What of the others, Lord? They hate me and would kill me.
> Must I extend a measure of compassion to them, too?
> It's too hard, Lord. I can't do it without Your help."

Loneliness

Which one among us has not experienced loneliness? Perhaps it's during a physical separation from family or a loved one. Maybe you feel it when you're in a large group or a big city and sense that you know absolutely no one. It could happen on the first day after leaving home to attend school or take a new job. Loneliness often strikes after the death of someone especially close. You may experience it in a quiet church while feeling God is no longer present to you. All of us have felt this aloneness at some time.

John Dunne wrote, "No man is an island, entire of itself." To me, loneliness has been an infrequent but distressing emotion. I hate to feel cut off. Some private moments of loneliness have brought me to tears. At other times I feel gripped by panic. I must find someone to connect with! Even though these incidents are few and far apart, they leave me feeling most uncomfortable.

How lonely Jesus must have felt when he began His public life by going into the desert for forty days. In the Garden of Olives and while hanging on the cross He was desolate. His friends had run away. Even His Father had left him.

"My God, My God, why have you abandoned me?" Christ asked. (Matthew 27:46)

When I start to feel lonely and sorry for myself, I think of Him hanging on the cross, awaiting death by Himself.

> "Father God, I pray.
> I keep the TV on, the stereo blasting.
> That helps me ignore the fact that I am by myself.
> I am often afraid to be alone, even with my own thoughts.
> On some level I think I am worried that I may die alone.
> I find my loneliness may really be selfishness.
> When I reach out to others, my isolation fades away.
> Lord, help me to rid myself of self-centeredness and to feel Your Presence."

The Big Mistake

Making "The Big Mistake" can haunt us for the rest of our lives. *What am I talking about?* The failure to study hard in high school that keeps you out of college. The teenage fling that produces an aborted fetus. Marrying the person everyone said was a loser and finding out they were right. Getting trapped in a dead-end job that offers few options for growth. A DUI arrest and conviction. Dependency on drugs. A living-on-the-edge lifestyle that results in a crippling accident. The list of potentially *big mistakes* is endless.

Depending on the gravity, the big mistake can be a life-altering event. A future of great promise turns into hopeless despair. A life of growth and productivity becomes filled with mediocrity and sullen despondency. A cheerful outlook turns into grim resignation.

Thanks be to God, I have not fallen into the *big mistake* myself as yet. Little mistakes? *Yes.* I find it is much easier to regain my footing after a *little mistake*. But whether we make the *big* or *little mistake*, how do we get back on track?

I turn to God first for help in making decisions. Next I seek advice from trusted friends I know will tell me the truth even though it might be painful. I have always believed that a decision carefully thought through and prayed about usually turns out OK.

> *"Father God, I pray…*
> *The road of our life's journey is strewn with potholes.*
> *Especially when we're young, terrible trouble can befall us.*
> *My ego and stubbornness lead me to the brink of disaster.*
> *I don't want advice. I've made up my mind about what's right.*
> *No, I must try to discern Your plan for my life, Lord.*
> *Help me to humbly accept Your direction.*
> *Protect me and my family members from making 'The Big Mistake.'*
> *And if we do, help us to recover quickly."*

The Hospital Waiting Room

I waited for each of my six children to be born. I sat in the lounge during a couple of my wife's surgeries. Yes, I've had some experience with hospital waiting rooms. Like many before me, and since, I have shared nervous laughter with other expectant fathers. Everyone knows that childbirth is a natural process. It is often long and arduous for the mother, but things usually turn out OK. We breathe a sigh of relief when the doctor comes out and says, "Mother and baby are doing just fine."

There is always a little cloud of doubt, though. Everything *should* turn out fine but…what if it doesn't? Anxiety builds as time passes. Why haven't they come out to tell me something? Is there a complication? When my wife recently had a hip replaced, the doctor said beforehand, "You should understand there is always a risk of death in major surgery." That was fairly sobering, to say the least.

My life seems to have lots of little moments of anxiety. I worry about things. Most of these events I can't control. I find it is very hard for me to put my total trust in God's plan for my life. Of all the virtues, trust is the most difficult for me. My failure to trust probably relates to ego and a strong desire to be in control of my own life. Do you feel the same way? What can we do to correct this flaw? Pray!

> "Father God, I pray.
> I swagger through life believing I am the master of my fate.
> Success is mine while mistakes are the fault of others.
> When faced with uncontrollable events, I become anxious.
> 'Should I turn to God? How do I trust someone I cannot see?'
> The Lord says, 'Relax…I love you and want the best for you.'
> Intellectually, I find this a comforting proposition.
> But from a feelings perspective, I encounter great difficulty.
> Help me, Lord. Trust is very hard for me."

The First Tee

Several of us play golf together regularly. The first match each spring is quite an event. After the winter layoff we all become reacquainted with our game at the driving range. Most of us, in a candid moment, will admit that our swing did not improve over the winter. But as we stand on the first tee we visualize that this day will be different from the past. Instead of muffed swings and errant shots our drives will be down the middle, followed by a second shot to the front of the green, a classy chip shot, and two putts for a bogey. This optimistic visualization usually disappears early in the round. Each of us is a year older, less flexible, and not as athletic. Our flawed swings rapidly reappear. We reset our objectives; maybe we can finish the nine hole round in less than fifty strokes.

My golfing experience is similar to the Lenten season. Each year on Ash Wednesday I promise that I will use these forty days to renew my spiritual life. I will attend daily Mass, read Scripture more faithfully, and give up some favorite food or drink. My zeal lasts but a short time. It's too tough to get up every day for Mass; things I promised to give up are served to me and I consume them eagerly.

I am like the seed spread near the footpath. Grain quickly sprouts but is then choked out by the daily cares of life.

> "Father God, I pray…
> This time, things will be different. Mark my words!
> I know covenants made this year will not be abandoned.
> This is the year of promises kept, of pledges fulfilled.
> In the wink of an eye my weak human nature emerges.
> All that I said I would do crumbles into dust.
> Why am I so weak, Lord?
> I am discouraged with my failure to be faithful to You.
> Please give me the graces I need to fulfill my promises."

My "Geezer" Friends

I have a number of male friends all about my age. Our wives get together once a month for card games and conversation. The guys take this opportunity to have dinner and then see a movie. During the long daylight hours of summer, we often play a twilight round of golf. Each man is unique in background, profession, interests, and opinions. Still, we seem to have an easy and compatible group. Each of us has irritating traits, but the others seem to overlook these little foibles found in others. We genuinely enjoy one another.

Dinner conversation often turns to the latest problem being experienced with hearing aids, joints, or prostate glands. A few of us are starting to admit that we're not as strong as we used to be. Our stamina is going, too. Some of the fellows say that nine holes of golf are enough for them. I totally agree; physical things are changing.

While the word would never cross their lips, on some level all these guys love one another. I have witnessed genuine care and concern being offered from one person to another. If any individual faced a crisis, I believe every man would step forward to help. Love: wanting what is best for another person—these guys demonstrate this feeling on a regular basis. What a wonderful relationship we have!

I am tremendously grateful to have these friends.

"Father God, I pray…
It is said that a true friend is a rare gift.
I've always envied those surrounded by friends.
Males especially don't form these bonds effortlessly.
Our emotional makeup does not permit easy relationships.
Help me, Lord, to overcome these macho feelings.
Let me be more caring, open, and loving to my male friends.
They are my brothers, after all."

My Brother

My brother, Dick, is ten years older than I am. When I was seven, Dick was preparing to fight as a soldier in World War II. His first action was the Battle of the Bulge. During his service he was awarded the Bronze Star for heroic performance. Other than reading the medal citation, I know very little about Dick's involvement in the war. He has never shared the details. I think that is perfectly OK.

Being more aware of our family's privation during the Great Depression, Dick has always been quite conservative. He seems to have sought stability and permanence in his professional life. After the war he finished his education and joined the U. S. Geological Survey. He rose through the ranks of that organization, continuing employment with them until his retirement. He was a recognized expert on riverbed sedimentation. After retiring, he was a professor for a few years. He authored or co-authored several scholarly articles and books. Personally, he is smart, funny, very committed to his religious beliefs and practices, a devoted husband, father, and grandfather. If he wasn't my brother, I would like to have him as my friend.

He and his wife have lived in Denver for many years. We have never had the opportunity for frequent interaction because of distance. But he has been a wonderful brother to me. I have always looked up to him. I know he loves me and I love him, too. We're both old men now. I wish we could have spent more time together.

"Father God, I pray…
Sometimes we forget how important family is to us.
We may grow up as sibling rivals; circumstances separate us.
As we mature, we come to understand fraternal bonds.
Our common heritage helps to bring us close together.
Lord, how lucky I am that You gave me a big brother.
Please bless him always with a happy and holy life."

My Sister

Ruth Anne Hadley Schlemmer was my sister. She was the classiest lady I've ever known. Ruth was thirteen years my senior. She was like a second mother when I was little. She was extremely bright, articulate, well read, an excellent writer, aggressive, and polished. Had she entered the workplace in the 80s or 90s…instead of the 40s…I'm sure she would have risen to senior management positions. As it was, she became the executive assistant to the chairman of a Fortune 500 company. She was some kind of woman.

Her husband, Don, died suddenly in the late 1970s. Ruth faced a difficult financial situation, with two kids still in school. Yet even in her grief she developed an action plan and executed it. The result: A second career providing financial security and a life of active leisure in retirement. She used every minute of her time in wonderful pursuits of adventure, education, and world travel. When at home, she became a master quilter and outstanding gardener. There was nothing she couldn't do. She was the perfect hostess and the epitome of grace and charm. I "rediscovered" Ruth in my mid-forties. She became a pleasant companion for my wife and me as we traveled to new places. I came to love her very deeply as I got to know her better.

Ruth died in 1995 after a six-month battle with cancer. Her death caused me profound grief. I miss her so! Time heals all wounds but, ten years later, I still mourn the loss of this great lady.

"Father God, I pray…
I placed my sister on a richly deserved pedestal.
She was greatly admired by all who knew her.
I was not ready to let her go when You came to get her.
My spirit was shredded when I saw her moments after death.
Tears filled my life for weeks and months after her funeral.
She was in a better place, but I missed her human presence.
Help me, Lord, to have more faith in the Resurrection of all."

My Wife

Evelyn Josephine Wright and I were married on May 4, 1957. We had met at the University of San Francisco. It didn't take us long to recognize we loved each other. Forty-seven years later our love remains strong, even though it is changed. This woman has provided me with the greatest life any man could hope for. She doesn't like it when I call her "Saint Evelyn," but that is how I feel about her. How she has put up with my mistakes, moods, and foibles all these years is unfathomable to me. It is said that no one goes to heaven by his or herself. Evie has been dragging me along with her for a long time. She has done this with patience and love. It is the same way she raised our six children.

My wife is bright and thoughtful. She is also a little gullible. The family often has a good laugh at her expense but she never seems to mind, even joining in the mirth. She is particularly caring to others who are ill, frail, or hurting in some way. Evie always extends a helping hand to those who need assistance. Her children adore her. The girls consider her their role model for life. The boys think of their mother as a perfect Mom. Evie's life accomplishments are legion.

I had no idea what things would be like after marriage. We slogged along each day enjoying the good times, working through the difficulties, and enduring the crises. Of all the blessings God has given me, my wife has been the greatest. I could never have made it this far without her love and help.

> "Father God, I pray…
> Young love is full of sparkling hope and promise.
> I couldn't imagine a life ahead that was anything but perfect.
> Time brought days of sunshine and the elation of love.
> There were also dark days filled with gloomy clouds.
> By Your grace, Lord, our vows held us together.
> Thank You for bringing this wonderful woman into my life.
> She deserves every ounce of my love and commitment."

Praying the Rosary

One of the most "Catholic" of all prayers is The Rosary. Although Jesus' Mother is admired by Protestants and Muslims, only the Catholics seem to offer prayers of intercession to Mary. We believe that Mary was conceived without original sin (the Immaculate Conception). We also believe that Mary was taken, body and soul, to heaven upon her death. Called The Assumption, this is one of only two doctrines that have ever been infallibly proclaimed by a Pope.

For those unfamiliar, The Rosary is prayed while reflecting on five events in the lives of Jesus or Mary. There are 20 stories in all, divided between the Joyful, Sorrowful, Glorious, and Luminous Mysteries that are prayed on different days of the week. After some preliminary prayers, each reflection is pondered while saying the Lord's Prayer and ten Hail Mary's, followed by a short Doxology. A string of beads helps the person praying to keep track of the prayers. I carry a small rosary in my pocket every day.

People new to The Rosary often say, "I find it boring and I become easily distracted by the monotony of the prayers. I prefer to pray directly to Jesus." Fair enough. But I find it comforting to say to Mary, "I need help; will you please go to your Son and ask Him for me?" How can Jesus turn down a request from his Mother?

> "Father God, I pray...
> Jesus loved his mother, the Blessed Virgin Mary.
> Scripture reveals little of Mary; Tradition somewhat more.
> Of this we're sure: She loved her Son in life and in death.
> She cradled His lifeless Body after the Crucifixion.
> I ask that she hold me tenderly in her arms, too, Lord.
> I will repeat the Hail Mary over and over.
> Just like a child repeatedly saying, 'I love you' to Mom.
> Help me, Lord, to pray The Rosary with devotion."

The Telephone Answering Machine

What did we do before everyone had a telephone answering machine? I guess I just called back until I got through or gave up. I don't remember. Now I resent it when I don't reach a machine or an answering service. *At least I can leave a message, with hope that I will get a return call.*

Some people use the machines to screen their calls. Only the messages of interest receive a call back. When I was in charge of raising money for our new church building, a lot of people who knew what I was doing didn't return my calls. I felt like a bill collector.

I wonder if God has an answering service. If I pray while He is busy helping some poor people in Africa or having a staff meeting with His angels, do my prayers get recorded for later review? Of course, I am being facetious, but sometimes I do wonder. There are millions of people constantly reaching out to God with their prayers. The clamor of all these petitions arriving at God's office must be terrific. Maybe God says, "This guy always wants help but he never says thank you." Message deleted! Or, "I never hear from this guy unless he's in trouble." Fast forward to next message! God wouldn't do that to me...*would He?*

Kidding aside, I do want to believe God hears all my prayers. From a human perspective, I seldom get feedback. Yes, I ask for something and it happens. I beseech God to heal a sick friend and they become well again. But my other pleadings, Lord—are they heard?

> "Father God, I pray...
> When the roads are smooth, I often forget You, Lord.
> Why bother God; I have all I need and want.
> Even my prayer of thanks is deferred to another time.
> But when the way is potholed, I cry out for help.
> 'I'm in trouble and You must help me now,' I plead.
> God sighs and listens. He must be very patient, kind, loving.
> Even when I ignore you, Lord, please don't ignore me."

The Automobile Accident

You're a careful and defensive driver. You seldom drive too fast and you work at staying aware of those driving around you. Stop signs are always observed. You never run a signal on red. Tailgating? Nope, you follow the four-second rule. You are a "good" driver.

And then it happens. Without warning, you're involved in an accident. Not just a little "fender bender" with a dented bumper or creased panel, either. No, this one produces broken glass and mangled steel. It takes but an instant. Your car winds up facing the wrong way in a lane of on-coming traffic. The other guy's car is in an equally distorted position. After the first moment of disorienting shock you feel some pain in your knee and look down to see torn clothing and a little blood. There's a cut on your forehead, too. Everything happened so fast your mind cannot recreate the situation. Have you experienced a something similar in your life?

Sometimes our spiritual lives get involved in serious accidents, too. A sudden explosion of temper results in a violent outburst toward a spouse or child. God-profaning words may spew from your mouth when you're cut off on the freeway. Anger and hate well up against a rival who receives a promotion you deserved.

Our dark side is just below the surface waiting to destroy us. The devil is alive and well. Sometimes I carry him around inside me. I must fight against this evil presence every moment.

"Father God, I pray…
I like to think I lead a 'good' life.
Evil is suppressed; the devil's blandishments rejected.
Then, out of nowhere, darkness blots out the light.
An explosion of anger, hate, and venom consumes me.
My spirit is invaded with black, vile thoughts and deeds.
Lord, protect me from these crushing spiritual distortions."

Sitting on the Front Porch

Our neighbors in Southern California owned some beach houses on the Balboa Peninsula at Newport Beach. During the summer we would often rent one of the houses from them for a week or two. It was a great place for a family vacation, and everyone thoroughly enjoyed themselves. Especially me.

One of the houses was directly adjacent to Balboa Boulevard, the street running down the middle of the peninsula. While the kids were at the beach I often sat on the front porch of the house with an iced tea and watched the world go by. Here I saw every possible slice of life play out before me. Bikers rolling by in their leathers. Swimsuit-clad teenagers racing on their skateboards. Families on bicycles. Old couples strolling down the sidewalk hand-in-hand. Hot-rodders cruising the avenue. *Wow!* I enjoyed my time on the porch while spectating on the world. I would sit there for hours, loving every single minute. Every new passerby represented an interesting experience for me.

On vacation in Balboa I was allowed to be a simple spectator. Now I am called to more than passive people-watching. I see neighbors, friends, and family passing by. Some have difficulties, others are hurting, and a few are confused and misdirected. I must be the Good Samaritan and offer help. In this world, mere spectating does not fulfill the role I am called to. I must love, and help, my neighbor. To this God calls me in the most fundamental part of my being.

> "Father God, I pray…
> 'People watching' is fun; their antics and mannerisms amuse me.
> It's harmless enough. I watch and do not get involved.
> But real life does not work that way, does it, Lord?
> I observe injustice, inequality, unfairness, and prejudice.
> I would like to merely watch; after all, it's not my problem.
> Lord, I feel Your call to a make a more noble response.
> Help me to get involved and assist when and where I can."

Coffee and Donuts

After Mass on Sunday we usually have coffee and donuts served in the parish hall. While this is obviously not part of any religious ceremony, it certainly represents an important fellowship aspect of our church community. I enjoy greeting friends and meeting new members of our parish. The donuts taste pretty good, too.

One time we attended Mass in a new parish. We went to the parish hall for coffee after Mass, as usual. Since we were new, we decided we would keep to ourselves and see if anyone approached us. No one did. We were really disappointed. Now, as an "old timer" in my current parish, I am always on the lookout for people I do not recognize. Sometimes it may be awkward, but the newcomers are usually grateful for the contact. I always try to introduce them to several other members of the parish.

In Matthew, Chapter 25, verses 31–46, I am told that part of my judgment will be based on whether or not I reached out to strangers and welcomed them. Introducing myself to someone over a cup of coffee seems a pretty small thing. But I may never know how important this simple welcoming gesture might be to a stranger.

I should spend more time looking into the faces of the strangers I meet. I might recognize the face of Jesus there.

> "Father God, I pray.
> The time after Mass is often full of animated conversations.
> Having shared the Eucharist, we enjoy greeting our friends.
> We share stories of our too-full lives, things good and bad.
> We feel a bonding, a companionship, a robust level of contact.
> But what of the stranger sitting in the corner?
> Is he to be excluded from our circle of friends?
> 'Whatever you do for him, you are doing for Me.'
> Help me to be welcoming to strangers, Lord. They may be You in disguise."

Wealth

I have several friends who are very wealthy. I know these people to be smart, hardworking, ethical, and unpretentious. Yes, they drive fine automobiles and live in beautiful homes. But they do not flaunt their wealth. Of course I am not privy to the specific ways they deal with their money. Are they generous to charity, the arts, or other worthwhile causes? I don't know. I do feel quite certain that none uses his abundance to suppress others unjustly. In most cases I knew all these people before they were rich. I liked them then and I like them now, because they do not seem adversely affected by the wealth they have accumulated.

Scripture tells us that "…it is more difficult for a rich man to enter heaven than for a camel to pass through the eye of a needle." (Matthew 20: 24). The gospel commentary says this refers to a specific gate, the "Eye of the Needle," entering Jerusalem. A fully loaded camel could not pass through this narrow gate unless it was completely unloaded. So, too, the rich person must unload all the material vanities of life if he is to enter into the Holy City. When the apostles asked Jesus how any wealthy individual could enter heaven, Jesus replied, "All things are possible for God." (Matthew 20: 26).

I feel sure God is telling us that wealth is not bad *per se*. Money clouds our spiritual journey only if we use it incorrectly or selfishly.

"Help me, Lord, to have the right attitude about the degree of wealth that I possess."

> "Father God, I pray…
> I do not think You want us to lead unhappy lives.
> Having some level of wealth can make our lives easier.
> Yes, I must be attuned to the needs of the poor.
> I must be generous when assisting the less fortunate.
> I am always concerned about how much is enough to give.
> Help me to share more than just 'what is left over.'
> Show me how to enter the narrow gate to the place where You dwell."

Mail Delivery

Each day millions of pieces of mail are entrusted to the postal service for delivery. Have you ever considered what a phenomenal system must be in place to make this happen? We all know stories about lost mail. Yet virtually all letters, postcards, and parcels deposited in one location arrive at a different destination correctly and in a reasonable amount of time. Upon reflection, I find this to be quite remarkable. Plus, the price of postage for this service is relatively inexpensive.

I am not an apologist for the U.S. Postal Service. I'm fairly sure they have lots of inefficiencies and a bloated bureaucracy. But who can deny that the end result *is* spectacular? A letter from one of my grandkids gets dropped into a mailbox in White Plains, New York, and three to four days later it arrives at my home in Tualatin, Oregon. What a deal!

I also think about all the people in the world who offer daily prayers to God. Millions, maybe billions, of petitions are presented each day. Those praying have hope that God will hear their prayers and answer them. Jesus said, "Knock and it will be opened; seek and you will find; ask and it shall be given unto you." (Matthew 7: 7).

"I believe You, Lord. And, yet, I sometimes wonder if You hear my prayers, especially the ones that are muddled, selfish, and unworthy.

Lord, please send me *belief* for my unbelief."

"Father God, I pray...
My human mind cannot process God's infinite power.
I forever think about Him with a clouded, finite intellect.
I want my faith to be strong, to believe that He hears me.
But, I can't see Him and often there is no feedback.
Even in my faith I sometimes find a niggling doubt.
Lord, I need a lot of help with this aspect of my life.
Like Thomas, I need to believe, not be unbelieving."

Remodeling

A couple of years ago we bit a rather large bullet and decided to remodel our kitchen extensively. The project was expensive and disruptive to our daily lives. Fortunately, we had a reliable contractor who finished the job on schedule. When the work was finally completed, we were very pleased. Everything turned out wonderfully. The room looked terrific and its function was much improved. It wasn't enjoyable going through it, but the end result *was* worthwhile.

I find that my spiritual life also needs an occasional remodeling job. Improper attitudes, spiritual complacency, new versions of old sins, and a general lack of fervor can creep into my life over time. I say to myself, "The current version isn't so bad; I can live with it for a little while longer." I resist change because of the disruption I will experience in my present comfort level. I also know it will require a substantial investment to modify my spiritual direction.

The time comes when I can no longer avoid the problem. The *spiritual remodel* may take the form of a serious retreat. Sometimes a thorough examination of my conscience is a key component. Sitting on a beach with a yellow pad to record a firm commitment to change may help. An extended visit in a quiet church often works. What is effective for me may or may not be helpful to you, however. Remodeling is a matter of personal taste, after all.

"I need You to remind me when it's time for remodeling, Lord. I know You are the most reliable contractor I could ever hope to find, and I know we'll both be happy with the results."

> "Father God, I pray…
> Over time my soul can get dingy and drab.
> Just like a well-worn home, my spiritual life needs rejuvenation.
> I resist change, Lord. It will be inconvenient for me.
> Can't I just stay pretty much as I am?
> Jesus says, 'You must be holy as the Father is holy.' (Matthew 5: 48).
> OK, Lord. Help me turn to You as my remodeling contractor."

The Mountains

I can walk about sixty yards from my front door, look east, and there see Mt. Hood. My daughter once owned a Portland hillside home and could see Mt. Saint Helens, Mt. Adams, and all the way to Mt. Rainier on a clear day. Our vacation travels in Oregon have provided grand views of Mt. Ashland, Mt. Jefferson, and the Three Sisters. While traveling to California we have driven by Mt. Shasta—seemingly close enough to touch. In Alaska we visited Denali, officially known as Mt. McKinley. Hawaii introduced us to Mauna Kea and Mauna Loa. Foreign trips have permitted us to see The Remarkables and Mt. Cook in New Zealand, The Matterhorn, and the Swiss and Italian Alps.

These magnificent, jagged mountains have each struck my heart with awe. In my spirit resides a picture of every mountain I have seen. They are so massive and dominate the view for miles in every direction. Looking at a mountain is like watching the ocean surf pound a beach. No matter how long you stare, each minute seems to bring a different perspective, a new aspect that gives wonder. These colossal natural structures represent to me clear signs of God's power and might in His created world.

How can I help but fall to my knees and praise the Creator of this universe? I am so tiny compared to these mountains. And yet, my God loves me unconditionally with every fabric of His being. How can this be? How can a single individual be blessed with God's complete love? What can I possibly do to respond to this tremendous love?

> "Father God, I pray…
> God watches over and protects even the tiniest sparrow.
> How much more He must care for me!
> The mountains around the world rise to the sky.
> God's grandeur is in full view to all who merely look.
> Yet I am more important to Him than the largest mountain.
> I must prostrate myself to this mighty God who loves me so."

The Rivers

Oregon is full of beautiful rivers with exotic names. Umpqua, Nehalem, Siuslaw, Santiam, Calapooia, Klaskanine, Rogue, Tualatin and Willamette are but a few. The great American river, the Columbia, serves as the northern border of the State for about two-thirds of Oregon. These waterways are important in a variety of ways—including natural beauty, commerce, fishing, and electricity.

I love to stop by the side of the road to look down and watch these rivers flowing. Fallen logs, rocks, and the natural geographical descent create whitewater in many of the rivers. I am always impressed by the grandeur and power of the seemingly endless flow of water downstream. Nature is one of God's great gifts to mankind!

I find a life-lesson when watching the rivers. Even in small rivers, thousands of gallons of water pass by a given point every minute. It is a perfect metaphor for the continuum of human life. We are born, we live, our human life ends, and we pass on to immortality. Each of us is but a single molecule of water. Millions of others join us on this journey, swirling around trees, crashing over rocks, pounding into the shore. Eventually we are released into the vast power and tranquility of the ocean. This moving concept gives me great comfort. Life may be full of rough patches, but we find peacefulness at the end of the journey. God leads me toward immortal life with Him. *How wonderful He is!*

> "Father God, I pray…
> Lord, let me always keep my eye on the final prize.
> The River of Life seems full of unexpected dangers.
> I crash into rocks and swirl in eddies of uncertainty.
> I trust that You will lead me down the circuitous route.
> When my earthly life is over, release me into Your Presence.
> Let me experience the joy of eternal existence with You.
> My hope is in Your mercy to me, a sinner."

My Calendar Book

For about as long as I can remember I have kept a detailed calendar book. I pride myself on being well-organized. I consider my daily notations a manifestation of my personal discipline. When I was working, my daily log was extensive. Even in retirement, I keep my calendar up to date, but not with the same detail or precision. My wife occasionally mumbles something about "obsessive-compulsive," but I haughtily ignore such comments.

One time my calendar book was offered as evidence in a civil lawsuit. My recording about a series of telephone calls to and from one of the parties to the lawsuit created a timeline that proved helpful in the case.

"Well," I said, "you can't have much better control over life's events than that."

Personal control over life's events...*what an illusion!* Because I wrote down all that had happened in the past and what I planned would happen in the future, I felt I was in control. Scripture says, "Be watchful and pray, for you know not the hour when you will be called to account." (Matthew 24: 44). What would make me think I controlled events? *Do I foolishly think I can bargain with God about how things will unfold in the future?* This is nonsense! Trust is seriously lacking here.

This is another example of my wrongheadedness about life.

"Father God, I pray...
Lord, it is clear to me that I am a sinner needing Your mercy.
In some things, my sin is more egregious than ever.
I don't want You to tell me how things are going to be.
I reserve that control strictly to myself.
Halfheartedly, I pray, 'Thy will be done' in the Lord's Prayer.
Show me, Lord, that Your plan is what is best for me.
Teach me to willingly turn over all control to You.
Help me to trust in Your will."

The Cleaning Ladies

Recently my wife and I became convinced that our creaking bodies weren't up to the thorough cleaning the house needed periodically. Our excuse was probably a rationalization; we just decided to hire someone else to do the work we no longer wanted to do. We found two ladies who visit every other Thursday. Between them, they efficiently clean the kitchen, do all the bathrooms, vacuum the carpeting, dust, and take care of several other chores. My wife is pleased to have this service. I have another secret, too. A gardener comes once a week to take care of our lawn. My neighbors all do their own yardwork so I have some guilt—but not much.

I suppose mopping a dirty floor or cleaning someone else's toilets could be considered demeaning. In the past, people with means often employed servants to do menial chores. There may have been a great class difference between employer and employee. In reality, we are all the same—people with hopes, fears, frustrations, and obligations to family, friends, and neighbors. While some may not agree, senior business or government executives are no better than the lowliest worker in the organizations they manage. All work has dignity.

I was raised in a working-class family. Work was highly valued, not only for the money it produced but because it gave purpose and pride to our daily lives. Ditch-digger and company president both who pursue their vocations with integrity are equal in the sight of God.

"Father God, I pray...
Dirty fingernails and grimy clothes are a legacy of some work.
Sweaty, physical, and difficult jobs are filled by many folks.
Stooping, bending, lifting, and dangerous tasks must nevertheless be done.
Is this less valuable than work done while in a suit and tie?
I try to visualize St. Joseph's calloused carpenter's hands.
Teach me, Lord, to value the work done by all people.
Each of us is called to fulfill a vocation as best we can."

The Comic Strips

After reading the first section of the morning newspaper I immediately go to the comics page. I have my favorites—*The Wizard of Id, Dilbert, Pickles, Zits, Mallard Fillmore, Cathy, Baby Blues, Ziggy, Family Circus,* and *Mother Goose and Grimm.* On Sunday morning I still follow *Prince Valiant,* and the animals in *Over the Hedge* amuse me. I don't care so much for the comics that push a political agenda like *Doonesberry* and *Sylvia.*

The creators of these comic strips do a great service for us. Those who have time to read the paper often start their day with a hearty belly laugh—or at least a good chuckle. The cartoonists help us to head out into the world with a smile on our face and a little mirth in our hearts. This has a better effect on our mood than the crime stories and human failings found on page one, I'm sure.

I have an obligation to make people happy, too. All of us carry little jokes and amusing stories with us. It's fun to make people smile or even laugh. I'm not a contemporary Bob Hope, but I do try to put a twist on a story that elicits a chuckle from those I am with. I am absolutely sure Jesus and his apostles had plenty of good laughs walking along the pathways of the Holy Land. I believe our God is a happy God who enjoys seeing us in our moments of laughter.

God sometimes calls me to a ministry of mirth.

"Father God, I pray…
There's a lot of serious stuff I must deal with daily.
Earning my daily bread and fighting sin wears me down.
I need diversion from this human grind occasionally.
A simple joke or an amusing story can lift my spirits.
If I need this uplifting shot of humor, others must, too.
Lord, help me to be a 'minister of mirth' to my brothers.
Help me to inject a little joy into the lives of those I meet."

Our Family Scrapbooks

The first twenty-five years of our marriage is a blur to me. Establishing a career and raising six children did not foster a leisurely pace of life. As the kids grew, we took lots of pictures and accumulated class photos and other mementos of their various activities. Like most families, all this was deposited in large envelopes and shoe boxes for some later, as yet undefined, processing.

Around our Twenty-Fifth Anniversary my wife began sorting all this material and creating a scrapbook. This was a big job. I agreed to keep our scrapbooks up-to-date after she completed the first twenty-five years' catch-up, and I have kept that bargain. Now we have a series of scrapbooks containing pictures and other objects that chronicle the life of our family. I don't know what will eventually happen to the books. I hope someone will keep them to show to family members still to come in the years ahead.

I think this memorabilia tells an important story about the history of our family. It reminds the reader about happy times and the major events that shaped our existence. It represents the people and things we value. It records milestones along the paths of life for a group of connected people.

I feel an urgency to pass on to others things from the past that are good. Proper manners, civility, and "doing the right thing" is often lacking today. We old-timers must bequeath these mysterious values to others lest they become extinct and forgotten.

> "Father God, I pray…
> When a family elder dies, much history is often lost.
> I know so little about those who came before me.
> I should do my best to create a record of my life's span.
> It helps new family members to feel a connectedness.
> This history applies to more than my human activities.
> Show me, Lord, how to tell my family of Your importance.
> Help me to touch their hearts with stories of Your unfailing love for us."

"A Bottle of Wine, a Piece of Bread..."

Edward Fitzgerald wrote in *Omar Khayyám*, "A jug of wine, a loaf of bread—and thou." Does this imply that an idyllic setting for lovers is to share a glass of wine and a piece of bread? Simple things can take on a special meaning. When I was a boy, my mother would occasionally buy a bottle of sweet Jewish wine or *Tokay*. I would plead for a sip at special holiday meals. I also remember that when my father moved to California in the late 1950s he was delighted with the selection of wine available to him in restaurants.

My son-in-law, Karl, is a wine salesman. We sometimes purchase a case of wine through his company to have when we entertain. My "wine cellar" has a nice selection of reds and whites. We enjoy sharing a bottle of wine with our friends. A glass of wine often accompanies our own private meals, too.

Think about this. Both bread and wine are ordinary things. They have been around for centuries. Their cost is modest. Yet these basic commodities are the centerpiece for a profound event, the Eucharist. Through faith and acceptance of the scriptural words of Jesus, we believe the bread and wine are changed into the Body and Blood of Jesus Christ at Mass. This is a stunning revelation!

I must be reminded that the simple can become sublime.

"Father God, I pray…
Daily I consume bread in some form and wine as well.
They provide nutritional value and their taste is pleasant.
In a typical day, these items of food and drink are simple:
Morning toast, a midday sandwich, a roll with dinner,
A glass of red wine with pasta or white wine with fish.
But, this food and drink can transcend my daily life.
Bread and wine become the Body and Blood of Jesus Christ.
Eucharist, central to my belief, is God's great gift to me."

The Backyard Barbecue

As a young husband and father I learned to do some simple barbecuing. Hamburgers, hot dogs, and an occasional steak were my repertoire. The kids loved the grilled food and my wife was pleased to have a day off from cooking. There was just something about outdoor cooking that made the food taste better.

Over the years I have not advanced my barbecue skills very much. I have friends who do some fancy cooking on the grill. My son-in-law, Bahram, has three separate units for different types of food he prepares. Even though my selection of food is limited, the barbecued meal has a special meaning for me. I particularly enjoy cooking outdoors when we have a group of friends for dinner.

There is something symbolic, almost sacred, about a meal cooked on an outdoor grill. After His Resurrection, Jesus showed Himself to his apostles by preparing a barbecued breakfast of fresh fish and bread. The story in John 21: Verses 9–13 is full of meaning—and so much that is important in life seems to happen at mealtime!

May I make every meal a celebration of life.

"Father God, I pray....
So often my busy schedule forces me to eat on the run.
I wolf down my food so fast I can hardly taste it.
There is no time to savor pleasant aromas.
Food is not enjoyed; it is merely ingested for nourishment.
Now, I must slow down and take my time.
Meals should become a time for meaningful encounters with others.
These are celebrations of God's gift of life to us.
Help me to see the sacredness in meals shared with others."

Auto Repairs

I have spent a lot of money on auto repairs. Even the best cars have things that break, however. I'm not talking about normal oil changes and lubrication. Those are necessary to minimize the unscheduled repairs.

Some upkeep is minor. A battery wears out. A turn-signal quits working. A fuel gage malfunctions. Other things can be serious. A carburetor fails. The transmission starts slipping. A differential gear begins causing trouble. Major repairs are exasperating, time consuming, and expensive. It's easy to waste a morning, even a day, while trying to obtain a repair diagnosis and get the job underway.

Similar events—*called sin*—occur in my spiritual life, too. Attendance at Sunday Mass and receiving the Eucharist may immunize me a little bit from sin. But sins still have a way of invading my life. For them I need an expert mechanic and a shop where my sins can be fixed. I find that place to be the reconciliation chapel in my church, where I receive the Sacrament of Penance, sometimes referred to as Confession.

My sins are not private. They affect others. They offend every member of the Body of Christ. I can't apologize to each person individually, so I confess my sins to a priest, who represents all of them. As God's minister, he forgives my sins on behalf of all my brothers and sisters. He extends God's forgiveness to me, too.

"Lord, keep me faithful to the Sacrament of Reconciliation."

"Father God, I pray…
An examination of my conscience reveals my sins.
I find a way to offend God and my neighbor too often.
No one knows but God; I will pray for His forgiveness.
And yet, I am part of the Mystical Body of Christ.
My sin offends all the other members.
I must seek forgiveness in the Sacrament of Reconciliation.
Lord, please be merciful to me in spite of my failures."

Pentecost

Fifty days after Easter we celebrate Pentecost. We hear the story of the Holy Spirit inspiring the disciples of Jesus to bravely preach to the world. Because Scripture speaks of "tongues of fire" that descended on the heads of the apostles that day, everything surrounding the celebration is fire-red. There are red vestments for the priest and red altar cloths. Even lay people are encouraged to wear red clothing to church that day. All of us are waiting to be touched by this holy fire. We acknowledge the Spirit's Presence with us even today.

Sometimes it is hard to accept that the Holy Spirit is still watching over the Church. Christ said to Peter, "You are the rock upon which I will build My church, and the gates of hell will not prevail against it. I will be with you for all time, even to the end of the world." (Matthew 16: 18-19). Jesus said it; we believe it.

"You sent the Holy Spirit, Lord, to protect us. But where was He when we started to have a drop in priestly vocations? Where was He as the ranks of nuns plummeted after Vatican II? Where was He when the American church was rocked by sexual abuse scandals? Where was He when the soul of the European church collapsed in the last decade? I want to believe, Lord, but I can't find evidence that the Holy Spirit is still here."

My clouded, finite intellect is filled with doubt. What a mistake! I cannot decipher God's plan for His Church on earth. I must accept God's promise that the Holy Spirit will be with us always.

> "Father God, I pray...
> For years, my church has been battered like a ship in a storm.
> Priestly vocations are drying up; what will we do?
> Nuns are virtually gone; who will teach our children?
> The European church is a shell; are any Catholics left?
> Thousands of children abused; how did this happen?
> The Lord said, 'You will be persecuted for justice's sake.'
> Help me to see the Hand of the Spirit in today's Church Universal."

Summer Vacation

Most of us living in America work too hard. Hourly workers are routinely required to work overtime. Salaried people often put in fifty–to–sixty–hour weeks, and more. Yes, our productivity is higher than most places in the world. Our workers drive an efficient engine of commerce that is the envy of all. But, many are tired from this overwork. Precious vacation time must be used to recharge our batteries. When I was running my own businesses, I insisted that people take their vacation every year. Everyone needs a distinct change of pace to rejuvenate themselves. That was a good policy, most agreed.

Vacation time refreshes us emotionally and psychologically, as well as physically. Unrelenting labor affects our spirit as much as our body. Sometimes a long weekend of three–to–four days is all we need to come back to work with renewed optimism and a new spring in our step. Depending on our obligations at work, a two-week vacation may actually add to stress. Being away that long often results in anxiety about what will be piled on the desk when we return to work.

I don't need a vacation from my spiritual life. I do need occasional rejuvenation. A routine of prayer and weekly liturgies can sometimes leave me uninspired. I find myself going through the motions instead of connecting with God in private and community prayer. Visiting another church, seeking out a short retreat or Day of Recollection, or perhaps a spiritual book can lift me out of my reverie. Taking time for these, I soon welcome a renewed spirit of thanks and awe for my God.

> "Father God, I pray…
> Daily prayer and weekly Mass seem to run together.
> I say the words but lack intensity, focus, and feeling.
> The sacraments console me, but I still have an arid soul.
> Lord, remind me that occasional renewal is necessary.
> My weak human spirit has trouble staying in touch with You.
> Refresh me with Your love, patience, and abounding grace!"

My Women Friends

Over the course of my life women have had a profound influence on me. I'm not speaking of my mother, my sister, or my wife. In addition to these most special ladies, other women have helped, shaped, advised, or led me. A few were extremely influential, though I suspect some of them did not even realize the effect they had on my life.

Early in my career at IBM, Linda worked hard to help me succeed. Kathy has been an important colleague and friend since 1990. Neighbors in California like Catherine, Helen, Mary, Donna, and Briegeen taught me about courage in the face of difficult situations. Oregon friends Theo, Sheryle, Carol, Claire, Judy, Liz, Geri, Jeanne, and Lois showed me what hospitality, humor, and commitment were all about. These were all bright, caring, people—full of compassion for others. And there are hundreds others. My contact with some has been brief or occasional. Others I still interact with frequently. Indeed, I have become a better person because of my women friends. In a special way, I love each and every one of them.

Sure, there are plenty of differences between us. The *Mars and Venus* thing is well-chronicled, but our humanity makes us more alike than different. We have the same fears, hopes, ambitions, expectations, and disappointments. While our physical and emotional makeup is different, we strive for the same objectives in life. As the song says, "We are one in the Spirit."

"Lord, help me to respect and cherish all my female friends."

"Father God, I pray…
Lord, some of Your best friends were women.
They were an important part of Your public life and ministry.
You treated every woman with respect and compassion.
Your encounters with them taught us all important lessons.
Show me how to extend equality, as well as esteem, to women.
Remind me of the gift and importance of women in my own life."

Work after Retirement

I know people who somewhat envy my retirement status. "Everyday is a holiday to you," they say to me, or, "What time did you roll out of bed this morning?" I tease them about not having to fight the traffic, drinking a second cup of coffee while reading the newspaper, or my daily afternoon nap. Yes, I do have a good deal.

My skills and talents didn't disappear when I retired. God had given me these gifts to use in my professional life. I think He expected I would continue using them. Couldn't I help a young and struggling entrepreneur get his business back on track? Shouldn't I employ my organizational skills to assist an important parish project? How about tutoring the youngsters in third grade with their reading?

It is pleasant to think about our retirement. No more work. Our lives will surely be better with additional leisure time and freedom from employment responsibilities. But we're not ending something; we are merely moving to a new space. God tells us that our gifts must be used in different ways to build up the Kingdom of God. A gold watch doesn't let us off the hook. We must stick with it!

I can't really retire. God has too much more for me to do.

> "Father God, I pray...
> No more need to rise in the darkness to get to work.
> Cross-country business trips are a thing of the past.
> I have finally earned some time just for myself.
> 'No,' says the Lord, 'I have many things for you to do.'
> I rebel: 'God, let me relax and enjoy my retirement time.'
> He responds: 'The talent I loaned you must be put to use.
> You must find a place to employ what I have given you.'
> Lord, show me how to continue building the Kingdom."

Public Speaking

Some folks are terrified to stand up and speak to a group. They would prefer a root canal or surgery without anesthesia. People who are animated and articulate while speaking one-on-one can just freeze up when looking out over a sea of faces. I don't know what causes this, but I'm sure it is a *real* phobic phenomenon. I have stood next to people who broke out in a cold sweat and turned woozy when required to speak in a public setting. Their anxiety certainly elicits my sympathy.

We know of many people who have risen to the top of their professions because of an ability to speak forcefully and with conviction. William Jennings Bryan, Teddy Roosevelt, Adolph Hitler, Mary Baker Eddy, and Bishop Fulton Sheen were all spellbinding orators. They achieved their ends—*for good or evil*—by captivating their listeners with inspired ideas and speaking techniques. It has often been said that *what* one says is less important than *how* one says it.

Without courage to speak, we miss opportunities to do good in our corner of the world. We can't share our civic, political, or religious convictions effectively without stating them publicly. To those in dread, Jesus said, "Do not worry about…what you are to say. For the Holy Spirit will teach you at that moment what you should say." (Matthew 10: 19-20)

Give me strength, Lord, when it is my turn to stand and speak.

"Father God, I pray…
My neighbors ask me to represent them at City Hall.
Our pastor wants me to address the assembled church.
I am invited to share my ideas at a local service club lunch.
This causes a knotted stomach and nervous anticipation.
Fear is assuaged by careful preparation and practice.
Lord, help me to say the right things in a convincing way.
Show me how to share my thoughts and inspire my listeners.
Let me represent Your viewpoint in the forums I will address."

My Mother and My Father

Fred A. Hadley and Gladys Eugenia Bingham were married in 1919. Dad was twenty-five; Mom was eighteen. She converted to Catholicism before their marriage. My sister, Ruth, was born in 1921. My brother, Dick, was born in 1924. I came along in 1934. When I was five years old my parents separated and subsequently divorced. I never knew the reason. I suspect much of their friction was economic. Dad's tire business went bankrupt in the Great Depression. Money was probably always an issue.

Mom was a dominant woman and tough as nails. She was always figuring out a way to support us with various ventures. She was a wonderful seamstress and made clothes for many important women in Minneapolis. I recall that she was not a happy person. She was also beset by many physical ailments, but she always kept on going.

I hardly knew my Dad. He was gone by the time I started to remember things. He would send me occasional letters, but I had virtually no contact with him. I presumed that, in contrast to Mom, he was laid back and probably lacked a strong character.

In the late 1950s Mom and Dad remarried. I guess they felt it made sense to live out their lives together. Dad wound up caring for Mom during her protracted final illness. She died in 1964. Dad died the following year of prostate cancer. I got to know him at the end.

With You, Lord, this man and woman co-created me. Thank you for their lives. Please bless them with eternal happiness.

"Father God, I pray…
You brought together two simple people to love each other.
They both struggled and tried to do their best in life.
Their lives were not filled with many happy moments.
There was heartache, were difficult times, and many wounds to bear.
Please be gentle with them now as they rest in peace in Your eternity."

A Teenager Learning to Drive

My eldest daughter, Eileen, was probably about sixteen when she began learning to drive. Driver education programs were not as prevalent then, so it was up to me to instruct her. I was driving an AMC Gremlin stick shift at the time. Our first lesson was conducted in the church parking lot on a quiet Saturday afternoon. Imagine an adult and a youngster both feeling high anxiety and full of tension. *What a sight!*

My attempts to be a dutiful and patient father lasted about thirty seconds. As Eileen struggled with gear-shifting and the clutch, I could hear my voice rising as I gave her new instructions. For her part, I could see the glistening perspiration on her forehead and upper lip. We were doing our best but it was not a warm and fuzzy moment. Within weeks, however, she was driving well and became a great help to her mother in delivering the younger children to their various activities.

Parents often have difficulty exchanging ideas calmly with their children. "Teachable moments" about life's events often collapse into shouting matches or sullen silence. Even when love is present, it is easy to fail when communicating. This is true for parents and children, bosses and employees, neighbors and family members.

My communication with others needs to be loving, patient, clear, and full of integrity. "Help me, Lord, with this tough task."

> *"Father God, I pray…*
> *I am speaking with someone I love; I seek the best for them.*
> *They love me in return and want to hear my ideas.*
> *Then something happens along the way; communication ends.*
> *Words, once loving and patient, turn mean and sour.*
> *Common ground, once broad, becomes shriveled and narrow.*
> *I don't want this to happen, Lord, but too often it does.*
> *My human weakness creates heartache for me and others.*
> *Please give me the grace to always speak lovingly."*

Baby's First Steps

First they pull themselves up on a convenient table or couch. Then they let go and plop on their butts. Pulling up is followed by walking around the table, hanging on. Finally, with family cameras nearby, baby takes a first step or two. It marks a big passage in the life of the child. Baby has taken the initial step towards eventual independence.

Sometimes this new skill can lead to danger. Our belief in Guardian Angels was reinforced as we watched our kids fall while learning to walk. Somebody *had* to be looking out for them.

Think about your own spiritual maturity. Somewhere along the way you began to develop a sense that life has some meaning beyond your own cocoon. You weren't sure where this feeling might lead. Like baby, you pulled yourself up on a nearby anchor. Cautiously, you examined this new idea. Eventually you got your legs underneath you. From then on, you began to create a relationship with God. How did this turn out for you? Did you experience some falls from grace? Did some Guardian Angels help you with the rough patches?

As a child I thought I had a connection with God. A sense of guilt and fear of a *Just God* kept me relatively focused as a teenager and young adult. It wasn't until some time later that I understood what kind of life I was being called to live. Understanding and execution are two different things, however. I find there can be a wide gap between knowing *what* to do and actually *doing* it. And it doesn't get easier with time.

> "Father God, I pray…
> Throughout my life, I struggle to walk in Your light.
> I know what it means if I live in Your grace daily.
> Like the infant, I must work hard to stay on the path.
> Just when I learn to step toward Your loving arms I fall,
> Sometimes hard and far, injuring my spirit.
> When I am flat on the ground, send a Guardian Angel.
> I need help to walk hand-in-hand with You."

Elation!

You hit the jackpot in Las Vegas. Your candidate wins a close election. The promotion you were hoping for comes through. Your college football team is invited to a bowl game. Your child is selected as a National Merit Scholar. A grandchild is born. You pass a serious medical test. A long-lost friend pays a surprise visit. Things like this give you a sense of euphoric happiness. You are elated!

The opposite of elation is desolation. Negative events lead us to a state of deep depression. These contrary emotions look like a pattern on an oscilloscope. Across our spirit we can feel the up and down *sine wave* model as we lurch between highs and lows. When we are younger and less mature, we ride these waves to the highest peaks and the lowest troughs. Maturity is when we dampen these "up and down" cycles. We don't get so excited when good things happen or so depressed when bad things occur. We begin to understand the biblical passage, "This, too, will pass." (Mark 14: 31). Nothing ever stays the same. Be pleased when things go well; be stoic when things are not so well.

My spiritual life is a mirror of these human emotions. When I feel close to God I must guard against thinking *I have it made*. Keeping the Lord in sight requires paying constant attention and prayer. When sin overtakes me and leaves me desolate, I can't throw up my hands in surrender. I must seek out the Sacrament of Reconciliation and trust in God's mercy toward sinners like me.

"Lord, I need your help to modulate both the peaks and valleys of my spiritual life."

> "Father God, I pray...
> As I age, I keep my enthusiasm under control.
> I feel depressed sometimes but try to keep it well in check.
> Over the years I have felt Your constant care for me.
> I know You love me and want what is best for me.
> I also recognize Your tender mercy and forgiving heart.
> Lord, help me to stick with You through the ups and downs of my life experience."

Rejection

It is like a spear stabbing through your heart. You hear words that say, "I don't love you! I don't want you! I don't need you! Get out of my life!" What can be more painful than total, utter rejection by another human being? Most of us do not treat one another with such harshness. If a relationship or friendship begins to fray, a termination can be achieved without such bitterness. Even folks who don't like each other will be reluctant to separate using such cruel words. It's like condemning someone to a life in solitary confinement.

Of course scalding words of rejection *are* used by some. A child lashes out at a parent. A man and wife who reach the end of endurance explode against each other. Former friends tear their relationship apart. How sad that we would treat each other this way.

Some of us reject God. We say, "Don't tell me what to do! I know what is best for me! I want You to get out of my life." This is called *sin*. Some sin represents a minor temper tantrum against God. It doesn't cut us off completely. Other sin is grave. It's when we turn our back on God, reject His sanctifying grace in our lives, and shout to Him, "Leave me the hell alone!" How distressed God must be when, through our own free will, we totally reject Him and His love.

"I have too much sin in my life, Lord. Give me the grace to be reconciled to You even after I have willfully rejected Your love."

> "Father God, I pray…
> I freely admit I don't like to be told what I must do.
> I want to decide what pleasures and actions suit me best.
> Jesus says, 'If you love Me, keep My commandments.'
> Sometimes I find that inconvenient or not to my choosing.
> I cry out, 'Leave me alone, Lord, Your will is burdensome.'
> Try as I might, I cannot stop sin creeping into my life.
> Lord, give me the grace that I might never totally reject You."

The Airplane Trip

Millions of people get into airplanes each day. These metal cylinders scream down the runway, gathering speed until they lift off and climb into the sky. Anyone who denies even a tiny bit of apprehension as the takeoff run begins is probably not telling the truth. Strapped into leather seats, we are totally in the hands of the pilots and the mechanics who checked the plane before the flight. The systems on modern jet aircraft are so complex that the slightest human error can cause disaster. Despite our worries, virtually every flight arrives at its destination safely. In spite of very infrequent catastrophes, we are reminded that air travel is safer than travel by car.

Why are we so willing to travel by air? We cannot deny there is the chance of an accident. Most of us know little about the aerodynamic principles that keep a plane in the air. Our knowledge about the hydraulic, electrical, and guidance systems is minimal. We have no idea about the skills of the pilot controlling this twenty-five ton piece of metal at 600 miles per hour. We must be cruising "the friendly skies," because we have faith that all the people and machines will work together to keep us safe and deliver us to our destination.

Faith: a belief in something we cannot see. Faith is central to our religious conviction. Have any of us seen God? How do we come to have faith? We cannot learn it or earn it. Faith is a gift from God. It can take us from here to eternity.

> "Father God, I pray...
> *The agnostic says, 'Show me!' He believes what he sees.*
> *The atheist says, 'I don't believe in God.' He also cannot see Him.*
> *I become impatient with others who do not share my beliefs.*
> *How can they not see what is so certain to me?*
> *Eucharist! Resurrection! A Triune God! All is so clear to me.*
> *Faith is not the product of an intellectual search for truth.*
> *Faith is a gift freely given to me by my God.*
> *'Help me, Lord, to cherish and nurture this precious gift.'"*

Wedding Anniversaries

The divorce rate in the United States is about 50 percent. One of two marriages is legally terminated. Many feel this way about marriage: "Let's give it a try; if it doesn't work, we'll get a divorce." What a distressing view of a sacred union! The family unit has been central to society for thousands of years. The increasing breakdown of the family unit foretells major societal problems in the near future. Single parents, homeless youth, and domestic abuse already afflict our cultural order. And the fallout from these events is getting worse.

The celebration of wedding anniversaries offers some antidote to this divorce situation. We recently attended the Fiftieth Anniversary of a couple we knew in college. Their celebratory party was a great joy to them, to their children, and their grandchildren. As importantly, it was a powerful witness to their friends and neighbors. Marriage *can* work! On our Twenty-Fifth Anniversary we restated our marriage vows in church before friends and family. We are joyful as our children begin celebrating milestone anniversaries, like ten and fifteen years. Whoever promised that marriage would be easy? Every marriage has ups and downs, rough patches, and difficulties. Commitment to the original vows is what holds things together. Grace can overcome all problems.

We have been married for forty-eight years. I hope to be around to celebrate our Fiftieth! Only God knows whether that will happen, and so I will leave it to Him.

> "Father God, I pray…
> We were young, in love, and eager to start life together.
> 'Sickness and health, richer or poorer, in good times and bad;
> Until death do us part'… seemed so far away in our 20s.
> Our vows were spoken with conviction, but without understanding.
> Now we have experienced so many years together.
> There were the highs and lows promised in our wedding vows.
> Euphoric days, sad days, happy times, disunity, and trouble.
> Lord, bless our commitment to our original vows and help them to last
>   forever."

The Capacity of a Child to Hurt

If you are a parent you know what I am talking about. All of us are occasionally susceptible to hurt feelings. The heartache can be delivered by coworkers, family, friends, neighbors—just about anyone. It seems that no one can offend us more deeply than our children. During teenage years, the natural desire for freedom and independence can cause a rebellious attitude, leading to hurtful confrontations with parents. Young adults often reject the life choices and values imposed on them. This can create a conflict so serious that lifelong alienation may ensue. As the old song goes, "You always hurt the one you love." Having your heart broken by one of your children is especially painful.

One of my teenage children got into a minor scrape with the law. Instead of turning to me for help and guidance, the child sought out the parents of a friend for comfort and direction. When I found this out, I was terribly wounded. *Why would my youngster seek someplace else to unburden the trouble? Was I not to be trusted? Did I have a reputation with my children for being too harsh or unforgiving? How could my kid possibly think these strangers would be more helpful than I would be?* When the truth finally came out, I went to my room, closed the door, and wept bitterly for a long time. I can hardly remember a time I felt so completely devastated.

By my sin, I wound God all the time. In spite of my rebellion He continues to love me unconditionally. I must try to do the same, especially when my feelings are hurt by someone in my family.

> "Father God, I pray...
> My skin is not thick enough; I am too easily offended.
> I will lash out—especially at neighbors, friends, or coworkers.
> But with children it is different. They can pierce my heart.
> Their actions sometimes cause devastating pain.
> Give me the grace of unconditional love even when I ache, Lord."

Habits

Every human being develops habits. Some of them are good; others are not so good. As one gets older it seems like more aspects of daily life become habitual. For example, a person may always get up at 7 A.M., shower, have breakfast of juice, cereal, and coffee, enjoy a mid-morning break, take lunch at noon, depart work at 5:30 P.M., and arrive home to watch the 6 P.M. news on television. After reading the daily newspaper and enjoying a favorite sports program, bedtime is 11:00 P.M. Boring? *Perhaps*, but routines like this are common and habitual for many. Habits provide stability for our lives. Just think of a time when events forced you out of your customary actions. Disruption of routine can be disconcerting and upsetting.

Habits can be important to our spiritual life, too. Do I have time reserved each day for prayer? Sunday morning is *always* set aside for Mass, right? I wouldn't think of approaching Christmas or Easter without having received the Sacrament of Reconciliation, correct? Is Scripture-reading part of my routine preparation for the weekend liturgy? Good habits are often hard to establish. Conversely, bad habits are easy to begin and difficult to break. It seems that our weak human nature forces us to work hard to create positive routines.

I have a few good habits but a ton of bad ones. A resolve to eliminate recurring negative actions takes a lot of concentration and work. I can't seem to do it without special grace from God.

"Father God, I pray…
Like most others, I am mostly a creature of my habits.
My life is glued together by my consistent routine.
Too much, Lord, consists of things producing a bad outcome.
A lifestyle established to find selfish pleasure and ease.
Not enough habit of prayer, self-denial, and care of others.
I confess my human weakness and a desire to change.
There is no chance of success, Lord, without Your help."

Rainbows

Some years ago my wife and I were driving through the Siskiyou Mountains, entering Northern California. The weather was unsettled with rain showers and periods of sunshine. The combination of these natural elements created a breathtaking series of rainbows. Usually only one rainbow is visible. We were observing new ones constantly as we proceeded down the freeway. I am told that no two people see a rainbow exactly the same way. The refracted light will look slightly different even to people in close proximity. The rainbow I see, therefore, is unique to my eyes. *This is incredible!*

There is powerful spiritual significance to a rainbow. In the Book of Genesis, Chapter 9, God promises Noah that the earth will never again be destroyed by a flood. As a sign of this, God says, "I set my bow in the clouds to serve as a sign of the covenant between Me and you. As the bow appears in the clouds, I will see it and recall the everlasting promise I have made." Many demand signs from God before they will believe in Him. The rainbow is just such a symbol.

Two things about this touch my heart. First, the rainbow I see is unique. Even though God has made a promise to all mankind, He loves me so much that the covenant is personalized just for me. Second, when a rainbow is visible I feel a connection back to Noah. It reminds me that my God is unchanging and almighty in His works. Those seeking a sign need only look east on a showery spring day.

"Father God, I pray...
The majestic rainbow provides a kaleidoscope of colors;
Sometimes bright and vibrant, sometimes muted and soft.
Every time I see one, I am reminded of God's promises.
He assured us of no more catastrophic floods.
But, more than that, He promised us a chance for salvation.
All that is required to obtain everlasting life is available.
The bow in the sky reminds us of all God's promises."

Where Do I Go From Here?

The conclusion of some activity often requires a review of what has been accomplished—a retrospective to determine success or measure potential failure. I have reached the end of what I planned to write in this little prayer book. After writing and rewriting more than 30,000 words, I find it nearly impossible to know whether the effort is any good or will be helpful to others. I suppose most authors feel that way at the conclusion of their work. Now comes the job of the brutally helpful but effective editors who will systematically point out shortcomings in grammar, syntax, and word selection. God must love them because they are so useful in teaching the virtue of humility to anyone who writes. Learning humbleness can often be full of pain, however!

My objective has been to prompt the reader to see God in life's common occurrences. Like the rainbows just described, I will find and see God somewhat differently than you will. My experiences and how I was affected by them won't be the same as yours. I encourage you to find the *little epiphanies* in your own life. God is present to us all. How that Presence is sensed will be different for each one of us. We all need to keep seeking God and then do our best to respond to His love for us.

With the time allotted to me still, I will try to follow Jesus' command: "Be good, as your Father is good." I have revealed enough of myself in the foregoing pages for you to know that won't be easy. Still, I'll do my best, and keep looking for those *everyday epiphanies*.

> "Father God, I pray...
> Why did I feel compelled to write these pages?
> Did I do it for myself, or will it touch some stranger's heart?
> We often do not know the people we affect for good or ill.
> I would feel blessed if You used me as Your instrument.
> Let this book find the hands and eyes of those who need it.
> I hope and pray that I could reach someone's heart.
> Remind me that it is not my words, but Yours that inspire.
> Help me now to lead the life I have described as my goal in this book."

To order additional copies of

100 Everyday Epiphanies

Have your credit card ready and call:

1-877-421-READ (7323)

or please visit our web site at
www.pleasantword.com

Also available at:
www.amazon.com
and
www.barnesandnoble.com
and
www.100epiphanies.com

Printed in the United States
68975LVS00006B/124-219